Getting Along
WITH MiSsy

An Entertaining Way to Cope

Getting Along
WITH MiSsy

An Entertaining Way to Cope

JANELLE SIMS

First Printing: 2019

ISBN: 978-0-578-22074-1

Janelle Sims
P.O. Box 7379
Pueblo West, CO 81007

authorjsims@gmail.com

This is dedicated to Greta's family

Preface

After I got over the initial shock of being diagnosed with a chronic illness, I did what I'd normally do: searched for books. As with many chronic illnesses, I found books that were scientific in nature and explained all of the aspects of the illness such as testing, causes, treatments, and symptoms. There were a slew of books about various diets and exercises known to improve the illness. There was even a good selection of personal stories.

However, after an exhaustive search, I couldn't find what I really needed. I was depressed and worried. I wanted to know what it was like to live with my condition but I did not want to be filled with dread or fear. I wondered what a day-in-the-life was like. Most importantly, I needed to *laugh*.

Having this illness become a part of my life was not chosen nor desired. However, through this series of short stories, it will be realized that it has brought life lessons, tons of laughter, heartfelt memories and most importantly, **a discovery of how to maintain my identity and not become consumed by my illness.**

May my lessons teach you, my method inspire you and my stories entertain you.

Story Order

My Roommate

I live with a roommate named Missy. To be honest, I don't like her and wish she'd move out, but unfortunately, eviction proceedings have been unproductive. She's the type of creepy person who slowly moves into your life without you really catching on and before you know it, you're stuck with her.

I wish I could say nice things about her, but I can't. She has obnoxious blond ringlets, crooked teeth, bad breath, frumpy clothes and an annoying personality.

Missy is controlling and abusive. If she wants to hang out at home and I want to go somewhere, she whines, hangs on me, screams at me and begs me to stay with her. She threatens that if I go ahead with my plans, she will go too and make me miserable. If I ignore her and try to get away from her, she'll always be there afterward; ready to beat me up and make sure I don't go anywhere else for a long time. I've tried standing up to her, yelling at her, and regaining control, but she is vindictive and ends up hurting me far worse than if I just did what she wanted.

Missy is a bully. She trips me and then laughs. She hides things where I can't find them. She jumps on my back when I'm trying to get things done and won't leave me alone. She finds it hilarious to cover my vision while I'm driving. She's awful.

Like a shadow, she insists on going with me everywhere I go. And I mean *everywhere.* Out with friends, on a hot date with my husband, and to my kids' events. She doesn't understand personal space and even tries to accompany me in bed and in the shower. Sometimes, she sneaks up behind me and squeezes me in the tightest,

1

most uncomfortable hug ever.

And all I know is that I don't like having her around, yet nothing I've done can make her go away. She has told me that she's not going anywhere and I just need to get used to it.

She likes when I limit my commitments and spend more time with her at home, taking it easy. She is beginning to understand that I'm still going to go do things with family and friends but she knows I will listen to her when I get home. I've learned that she often likes to tagalong with me, so I've introduced her to people who are close to me. I don't let her frustrate me when she trips me, or when she hides my things. I just know that's *her,* and I don't let her bring me down.

Don't get me wrong. Should she choose to move out, I will immediately help her pack her bags. But in the meantime, I'm going to try to focus on the positive aspects of having her in my life.

This isn't unlike other trials I've conquered in my life. Just a little background: I went blind in my left eye when I was three years old. I also suffered from linear scleroderma at the age of four, which caused the left side of my body not to develop properly. My left leg has low muscle mass and was a couple of inches shorter than my right leg. *This did not stop me from doing anything I wanted to do!* I was a concert pianist, a dancer, a singer, an A student, and could beat any girl or boy in a 50 yard dash! These things didn't stop me from driving a car, being on the swim team, dating boys, being a runner up in a beauty pageant or going to college. I was able to graduate from college, get married, have two children and be a successful teacher. (Okay, being blind in one eye means I can't use 3-D glasses so 3-D movies are out, but that's all!)

The point is, I learned to live with my blindness and little leg. I could learn to live with Missy, too.

Because Missy is merely: Multiple Sclerosis.

It was another illness that I had to conquer in my life. However, unlike blindness and a deformity that can be compensated for, Multiple Sclerosis is an active, life-long source of destruction with no end in sight. It literally has a life of its own.

Hence, my idea to personify MS into Missy. By separating her into a being of her own, I could try to control her.

I was able to essentially ignore my other health issues, but ignoring Missy did not work. If my legs were tired, I'd ignore her and keep walking. If she made me feel sleepy, I'd drink some coffee and get busy. However, the more I ignored her, the more vindictive she became. I suddenly started losing my vision in my right eye, which is the only eye I can see out of. Not being able to see is definitely one way to make me slow down.

But isn't this what it means when people say to stand up and fight *an illness? To fight* Cancer. *To fight* Multiple Sclerosis. *Be a warrior, a fighter. Doesn't that mean to not let it stop me? To be stronger than it is? Why doesn't ignoring it work?*

Once I realized this ignoring/fighting approach wasn't working....okay, I'll be honest. It took a doctor, a nurse, a

3

boss and ten members of my family and friends to make me realize my approach wasn't working. My illness was rapidly progressing and I was forced to leave my career. I'd been a 5th grade teacher for six years and I loved it. Having this rug dragged out from under me made me realize that my version of fighting MS was not working. So I adopted the saying: "Keep your friends close and your enemies closer."

Missy was definitely my enemy. I needed to get to know her and to figure out what made her tick. I needed to accept her presence in my life and learn to live with her ever-changing, manipulative ways. We'd have to communicate and compromise on the things we each want and don't want.

I needed to *get along with Missy.*

The "Mind Eraser"

Knowing what I know now, I'd had MS long before my diagnosis. But, I was a busy, active, working wife and mother. I didn't have time for silly little symptoms to stop me from what I needed to do. I'd notice fatigue or numbness here and there but I'd ignore it and continue with my life.

It was June 9th. My kids and husband and I decided to spend the day at a theme park. The kids were finally old enough to ride the thrilling roller coasters. We rode the "Mind Eraser." Twice! It's the kind of roller coaster attached from the top where the rider's feet dangle and swing. It had drops, loops and turns. I loved laughing and screaming as loud as I could, listening to my husband's profanities and glancing at my kids to see if they were terrified or exhilarated. It's one of the few activities we mothers can do that is "cool." I got to step out of the careful, keep-everyone-safe/calm role and show my kids their mother's wild side. We'd get off the ride and excitedly talk about our favorite parts and make fun of each other.

I remember riding ride after ride, even the water rides at the water park side. I remember feeling more tired than usual and definitely feeling woozy when I got hot. But, who cares?! I was there to have fun with my family! Push through it.

It was a fun-filled day. One for the memory books. In more ways than one...

The next day I noticed that my left hand was kind of numb and tingly. I couldn't feel textures or temperatures accurately. I thought, "Uh oh. I must have messed myself up on that rollercoaster. I should go to the chiropractor."

In the meantime, I tried remedies such as an anti-inflammatory and using magnets. Throughout the day, the feeling traveled up my arm. Throughout the weekend, the numbness and tingling spread down the left side of my body including my trunk, leg and even up my face. I went to the chiropractor on Monday. I told him about my symptoms and how I'd ridden a wild roller coaster. He "adjusted" my neck. I use "quotation marks" because I left his office disappointed. Although he thought he'd adjusted my neck, I'd never felt anything pop or move like usual. (I discovered later that he suspected MS based on my symptoms and was concerned that an adjustment could cause further nerve damage.)

By that evening, I was struggling with walking. I went to the grocery store with my husband and he noticed, with quite concern, that my left leg was dragging as I walked. I saw my primary doctor the next day. He sent me for a CT scan to check for a stroke and then for an MRI. I went back to his office the next morning for the MRI results. He sighed heavily and said, "According to this MRI, you either have Multiple Sclerosis or a brain tumor. We need to get you admitted to the hospital." I didn't know what Multiple Sclerosis was but I knew what a brain tumor was. My grandmother had died from one.

Within a couple of hours, I was admitted to the hospital and awaiting a neurologist. I was started on IV steroids. The neurologist looked at my symptoms and MRIs and confidently told me that I had MS. I was so relieved! It wasn't a brain tumor! Whatever MS was, would be fine. I could handle it.

That evening, my room was full of people: my doctor, two nurses and my husband. The purpose was to console me about my MS diagnosis. They had such sad facial expressions. My husband had tears. I, however, had my usual smile and positive attitude. I'd overcome other medical issues. Nothing had ever gotten me. This wouldn't either. I couldn't understand why everyone was so sad and worried.

That night, I researched and read all about MS on my phone from my hospital bed. I became educated about the different forms and various symptoms. I read about treatments for disease progression as well as symptom management. Still, it didn't scare me. I would fight it like I fought everything else.

Boy, did I have a lot to learn.

Little did I know that Missy had been along for the ride on that "Mind Eraser" rollercoaster. I'm sure she was excited about the symbolic uphills, downhills, twists and turns she was about to cause in my life. Funny, I don't remember buying her a ticket.

I'm so thankful that my last normal day was spent laughing and squealing and even cussing with my family. I will cherish that memory for the rest of my life.

A Long Summer

Immediately after my diagnosis, Missy hit me with a two-by-four upside my head. After I was discharged from the hospital after finishing steroids, I grew much worse. I became weaker by the day. I struggled to make my left leg lift, move and step. I began to lose what little muscle tone my left leg had left. I was given another course of IV steroids with home health. I couldn't stand up to shower. I couldn't walk without a walker. I even struggled sitting upright for very long.

I reached out on the Internet, to MS helplines, to friends with MS. Nobody could believe how severe this exacerbation was for me. I finally saw a new neurologist who explained it to me. The lesion in my cerebellum was very large and active and it had already caused severe nerve damage.

There was nothing left to do but attempt to recover. Our family vacation was scheduled at this time. Fortunately, it was to a small, quiet town in the mountains. Our timeshare unit was a full two bedroom, two baths with a kitchen and living room. I figured, if I could lie on a bed or couch at home, I could do it there, just as well. We moved forward with the trip.

The family enjoyed the local activities while I tried to improve function. I completed small exercises in bed in order to regain muscle. I rested and slept. A lot. Eventually, I tried taking small walks without my walker. My first goal was just to make it to the sidewalk. Each day I would try to go a little farther down the sidewalk. I wanted to see the mountains, feel the sun and breathe the mountain air. My family had to hold me up the whole way. They were incredibly supportive both physically and emotionally.

I did what I normally did to get through hard times. I poked fun at myself. We laughed together. The kids would join in making fun of me, challenging me to a race or threatening to leave me alone on the sidewalk. My husband, the I-can't-dance-nor-will-I-ever-try man, suddenly started joking about wanting to dance with me. He'd ask me to dance, and then laugh when I'd smile while flipping him the bird.

Some days I'd seem a little better. Then, I'd backslide. Two steps forward and one step back. I couldn't figure out what I was doing wrong. I knew I was suffering from some steroid withdrawal and that that was causing some of my lethargic, weak feelings. I tried eating certain foods and not eating others. I tried walking less. I tried taking cooler showers. I'd never tried to recover from something that didn't respond as I wanted it to. Everything I'd ever done was accomplished with my hard work. If I worked hard, did everything in my power to succeed, and didn't quit, I'd be successful. This approach didn't seem to be working this time. Alone, I cried. In front of my family, I'd smile and make them laugh.

By the end of our vacation, I was frustrated and depressed. Would I ever recover from the MS flare up? Everything I'd read said that people with Relapsing Remitting MS (RRMS) typically recovered from flares in days or weeks. I was going on months.

I went to the sidewalk for one more walk and that's when it hit me. I'd barely even made it to the sidewalk at the beginning of our vacation. I remembered where I'd started and how this time, I was walking the whole length of the sidewalk. I was still shaky and uncoordinated and in need of help, but I walked farther than I could at the beginning of our trip.

Not only had it felt like two steps forward and one step back, but it was toddler-sized baby steps forward. But it was still forward. I was nowhere near where I wanted to be nor where I thought I'd be, but I'd improved. I had to accept the slowness of the process. I had to accept that I'd have moments, even days, that I went backward instead of forward. I had yet to fully know and understand Missy, but I was beginning to learn her power and control and accept that my sheer will would not win this war.

Welcome to the Family

When I had found myself in the hospital with the new MS diagnosis, my daughter had been away at camp. She loved attending the camp for a week or two every summer, in the mountains complete with rock climbing, canoeing, campfires, and silly songs. It was her time to get away and be a typical kid. For the rest of the year, she was anything but typical. She had always been bright, even gifted. She was able to breeze through school curriculum very quickly and found herself as a freshman in high school at the age of eleven. Still, she wasn't satisfied. She began talking to the school administration about allowing her to begin college the following year at twelve years old. They agreed. Over the next four years, she not only completed high school, but she simultaneously completed a full Bachelors Degree in Sociology and graduated at the age of sixteen. So, for those precious two weeks each summer, I loved the idea of her being a carefree kid, putting on war paint and playing capture-the-mattress in the woods. I was *not* about to send word to her that I was in the hospital.

However, I was unable to drive to the camp to pick her up and attend the ceremony in which she'd be presented her unique camper award. Another family member went to get her for me, but before that person could explain why I wasn't there, her younger brother blurted, "Mom is in the hospital and she has Multiple Sclerosis."

My husband immediately brought my daughter to the hospital and she could see that I was still smiling, talkative and "okay." Knowing her, I'm sure she went home and researched everything about the disease. Once I was released from the hospital, she assumed all roles and responsibilities of the mother in the house. She cooked, cleaned, did laundry, and waited on me hand and foot.

She even tackled the task of grocery shopping for the entire family. She didn't need a shopping list because she had memorized all the items everyone liked and used. My husband dropped her off at the store; she walked in to grab a cart, and expertly walked up and down each aisle gathering everything we needed. She noticed people looking at her, fifteen at the time, and wondering why she was there by herself with a cartload of groceries. It's not a common sight. She even knew how to use coupons and price-matching. My husband met her at the check-out and helped her load the groceries into the car.

She was my thinker and doer. She stood at my door and offered to do anything and everything I needed. She never showed fear, sadness or worry. She didn't try to comfort me. She just wasn't "peopley," as she called it. She handled Missy joining the family by researching and psychoanalyzing our new house member and completing any job that needed to be done that Missy interfered with.

My son is three years younger than my daughter. He is also incredibly intelligent and ahead in school. He also has natural people skills. He always made friends easily and had a talent for knowing how to help people. He could figure out what they needed before they asked and would jump in to help.

When Missy moved in, he was my bodyguard and my companion. He wouldn't leave my side. He was content to lie next to me and watch hours of television. He helped me with physical therapy. If he saw that I needed to adjust a pillow, he'd instinctively jump up to help me with it. If he sensed that I was uncomfortable, he would problem-solve and do everything he could to make it better. He was my empathic, compassionate caregiver.

At one point, I was taking a disease-modifying drug that required me to give myself a shot in my hips, thighs, arms or stomach. I dreaded those shots. They burned and I would get big, red, sore welts that would last for days. My son always recognized when it was "shot night" and he'd greet me afterward with a candy bar and an ice pack. One night, I asked if he'd find something on TV to distract me while I held ice on my leg. I came out to discover that he had the beach volleyball scene from Top Gun ready for me to watch. Thatta boy.

My husband took on the "ball juggler" role. A wife and mother juggles various people, schedules and activities. When I went down, he jumped in to keep all the "balls" moving as necessary. He also comforted me the best he could.

I'll admit to having the serious conversation of allowing him to leave our situation. It wasn't what he signed up for, and I felt he deserved to go live the rest of his life without my being a burden.

One night, in the privacy of our room, I bravely brought up the subject.

I said, "Honey, you didn't sign up for the kind of life Missy is going to lead us to. If you want to leave, I understand. I don't want you to have to deal with this illness and me. I want you to enjoy your golden years. I want you to travel and have peace and joy. I'm serious. No hard feelings if you want to back out of this marriage."

He immediately responded, "Baby, my life is nothing without you. I'm not going anywhere. We're in this together. In sickness and in health. It's you and me."

Although I'd come to question his decision over the years, he never seemed to. He accepted having Missy join our marriage.

However, we had to adjust some expectations in our relationship. Instead of a hot date consisting of a fancy dinner and drinks, it instead might be cuddling at home to a movie. When he walks in the house after work, I've asked him to notice what *is* done instead of *not* done. There might be a mess in the living room, but notice the load of laundry I completed.

The whole family seems to accept Missy the way I do. They don't like her. They think she's unfair and mean. Sometimes they laugh at the things she makes me do. Sometimes they silently resent her for making all of our lives difficult. They know she has the potential to take me away from them, maybe not in death but in function.

But never once have they blamed *me* or gotten frustrated with *me*. They know it's all Missy's fault and they're allowed to hate her and even (mildly) cuss at her.

If they have ever felt sorry for themselves for having a sick wife/mother, they've never showed it. I'd like to think I'd be understanding, but I also know I wouldn't allow them to wallow in a self-pity party for very long. Life isn't fair. Suck it up. Party over.

It's as if having Missy join our family only strengthened

our familial bonds. We're on the same Anti-Missy team and together we will work to fight for as many incredible, lasting memories as we can create.

The Hot Tub

We'd lived in our modest home for seven years. It was only a starter home and we had lived there longer than we had planned. It just so happened there was a house right down the street that we loved. We put an offer on the house and put ours up for sale.

Buying and selling houses, things go right and things go wrong. There's the excitement of a new place and the sadness of leaving a house full of memories. It took a couple of months to get an offer on our house. Unfortunately, the inspection on the house we were buying didn't go as well as we'd hoped and the owner refused to cooperate. Suddenly, we were backing out of buying a house and trying to stop the contract on the one we owned. It all worked out but we were left feeling disappointed.

Why had it worked out that way? We had lost our dream house.

Eventually, we decided we loved our house enough to stay and make it the way we wanted. We put in beautiful hardwood floors. We had walls torn down to accommodate my newly inherited baby grand piano.

And most importantly, we custom designed a hot tub room. Hot baths, hot springs and hot tubs were my favorite things. I loved sitting in warm water and reading a book. We only had a small bath tub in which either my legs or my torso could be soothed by the warm water while the other would chill in the cold air. Sit up, scoot down. Sit up, scoot down. That's how I tried to stay warm in my bath. If we were going to make our house into our dream house, it was going to need a hot tub.

It would be a separate building behind our house. Its outside matched the main house's stucco and the inside was constructed of beautiful cedar. We installed a hot tub with therapeutic jets, a waterfall, and lights. It was a dream come true!

During the construction of the hot tub room, I ended up in the hospital where I was diagnosed with MS. Within a short time, I began learning of the various possible MS courses of progression, the symptoms and the ways in which to manage the disease.

Reading through material: *Hold up! What was that?! People with MS shouldn't sit in warm baths or hot tubs?!* Apparently an increase in body temperature can cause symptoms to flare.

Meanwhile, construction workers were at my house at that exact moment building a $15,000 hot tub room for me.

I was devastated. How was it possible that I was diagnosed with the *one* disease that would keep me from my very favorite activity? I understood that crazy roller coasters and sky diving might be frowned upon as a risk to one's MS, but a flippin' bath?! I could no longer sink into a relaxing, soothing tub of hot water and bubbles at the end of a long day? I wouldn't be able to enjoy the luxurious hot tub I was having installed.

I could see the blessing when it came to losing our dream house. It was huge, expensive and full of stairs. It was not the right house for someone who had Missy as a roommate. I felt God had saved us from a huge mistake.

It's too bad my roommate had a thing against hot water.

It's as if Missy said, "Let me figure out what Janelle enjoys the most and that will be the one thing I take away from her." I hated her.

At first, I was in denial. I'd be one of those people who weren't affected by the hot water problem. I sank into my brand-new hot tub complete with changing lights and pounding jets. It felt so good.

For a little while.

My left leg started to feel stiff. *Nah, it was my imagination. Just move it around. Get comfortable again.*

After a couple more minutes, my leg began to cramp. *Is this what they meant about hot water causing problems?* Grumbling, I got out. My leg wouldn't bend or move. I had to wait to cool off before I could try walking inside.

So, as I'd come to find out, ignoring Missy or fighting her doesn't work. One can't just overcome or conquer MS. We have to compromise and communicate. Missy and I began to do just that. I refused to let her take hot water from me. Instead, we compromised by lowering the temperature to slightly warm and by limiting my exposure time. Neither of us was ecstatic with this agreement but we tried. Missy is quite pushy; she'd threaten to hop in the tub and create spasticity if I took advantage of the situation. I paid attention and got out of the water before she could put on her swimsuit and bother me. There wasn't room for both of us.

Survivor

That summer I was diagnosed was a summer from hell. Between the flare up and the rounds of steroids, I was a wimpy puddle who could barely sit up. I did my best to get through small amounts of physical therapy several times a day. Otherwise, television passed my time. Since it was summer, my kids, twelve and fifteen at the time, were home with me. My daughter discovered all thirty past seasons of *Survivor* on Netflix and the binge-watching began. Episode after episode, season after season. I should explain that my kids and I don't just watch TV. We discuss it. We constantly pause the show to pose questions and voice opinions. (My husband strongly dislikes this. He wants us to shut up and watch the show.) But I love the interaction. They're old enough to strategize, to talk about social acceptance and to evaluate personalities. We'd all pick our favorites and get nervous during each tribal council waiting to see who would be voted off. Watching *Survivor* was much more than just watching a show. It was an experience.

We began making *Survivor* references around the house. My physical therapy became "Today's Challenge" and I'd get a reward "worth playing for" at the end. Sometimes we'd all perform physical therapy to see which one of us could "win immunity." We'd hum the theme song while doing chores around the house together.

It was a *Survivor* summer. It was the first time I was unable to be the mother my kids were accustomed to. The mother who could go and go and who did many motherly tasks for them. At this point, I could barely walk or sit up. They had to care for *me* for a change. Much like the contestants on *Survivor* who were thrust into a new and difficult environment, together we had to discover how to acclimate, to stay strong both physically and emotionally, to try tasks we'd never tried and support each other.

I cried a lot. I was miserable but I was also scared. Missy's world was new to me. Nobody could tell me if I'd get my strength back, if I'd walk again, or if I'd get the feeling back on the left side of my body. Improving, *surviving*, became my full time job. Challenging myself to do a bit more each day was my battle. Setbacks became pivotal. One day at a time was key.

Guess what? Our alliance made it to the end. My kids helped me fight Missy every single day. They helped me learn to walk again. They cheered me up and cheered me on. Our bond, mother and children, couldn't be broken. We didn't receive a million dollars but we gained priceless memories.

Survivor's motto is "Outwit, Outlast, and Outplay." How coincidental that those three things are what it takes to survive Missy. It isn't a fight. It's the ability to win through will and determination, clever strategy, and relationships forged with known enemies. Therefore, I am a survivor.

Don't Be a Hypocrite

My first major MS episode, the one that led to my diagnosis, began in June. This meant that, as a teacher, I had the rest of the summer to bounce back and get ready for another school year. I use the term "bounce" to elicit humor. One with MS does not bounce, nor is it possible to simply bounce back to health. I spent that summer slowly learning to walk again. I began to understand the concept of energy conservation. I even researched tips from other MS educators when it came to setting up and running a classroom.

At this point in my career, I'd been teaching 5th grade for 5 years. I loved it and I was good at it. I worked in a great school with other teachers whom I respected and loved. I sincerely cared about all 90+ of my students each year. I worked to distinguish the strengths and weaknesses of each child so I could help them grow. I loved fifth graders because they were old enough to understand my sense of humor and to work independently yet young enough to still enjoy coming to school. I taught my favorite subject all day: reading. I loved helping weak readers excel and I tried to inspire all my students to discover a love for reading.

As the start of school approached, I had the harsh realization that I would need the help of my walker to get around the big building.

How embarrassing. What would the other teachers think? What would the students think?

Before school began, I went to set up and decorate my classroom. I enlisted the help of my husband and children. My poor family. In the past they'd all helped with decorating, cleaning, grading papers, cutting out shapes and all varieties of teacher's duties. I relied on them even more this year. Since nobody else was at the school yet, I didn't hesitate to use my walker. My classroom was the farthest one from the front door. I made my way back to my room and began delegating duties to my family members. I used to pride myself as being a teacher who moved throughout the classroom all day. I knew this would need to change, this year at least. Instead of setting up my desk and my reading table on opposite sides of the room, the way I'd always done, I set them next to each other on one side. I bought a stool to sit on at the front of the classroom. I began to see how I could make this work.

Except for the walker. I didn't want people to see me using it. And then it hit me. What a hypocrite I was!

The majority of my students required accommodations. They needed math charts, reading assistance, extra time and extra help. They learned that they could do *better* with this help. Could I walk from the front door to my classroom without my walker? Yes. But I could do it *better,* more easily and more quickly with the walker. If my students could accept help to perform better, I should too.

So I decided Missy and I would start the school year with the use of the walker. I would take the opportunity to educate my students about MS and about my need for the walker.

That day, after my room was set up and it was time to lock up and leave, we walked toward the long, wide hallway leading to the front door. My teenagers suddenly said for me to "Hop on." Laughing, I sat on the seat of my walker, lifted my feet, and they began running and pushing me down the hall! We were all laughing and I saw my walker in a different light. If my own kids could be light-hearted about it and understand why I needed it, I knew my other kids would, too. I couldn't expect them to accept help if I couldn't do so myself. Missy wouldn't get the pleasure of embarrassing me about a walker anymore.

I've always wondered if my administration ever watched the surveillance camera footage of my walker ride down the hall. If so, I hope they found it a funny sight!

The Walk of Shame

It was the summer before my diagnosis. It was before I even had a clue what MS was. My husband, kids and I had planned a family vacation to Las Vegas. It's a place my husband and I had visited together several times before. We wanted our teenagers to see the sights. And I don't mean the mostly-naked, things-popping-out-of-places sights. My daughter was old enough to see those billboards and not think twice about them. My son was young enough to see those billboards and look away in embarrassment. We wanted them to see the buildings, the lights, and the excitement. We knew they'd enjoy the street performers, magicians and acrobatic acts. Even the architecture and decor is unlike anywhere else.

But most importantly, we were going there for a wedding. My husband and I had gotten married eight years before in a ten-minute ceremony along our local riverwalk. It wasn't our first marriage, so we didn't want or need the pomp and circumstance. My parents and young kids were the only attendees. I'd spent hours coming up with vows, readings, and a ceremony procedure. However, when the time came, it was nine minutes too long. I'd felt such an urgency to just get to the point of declaring us married. *Just tell me he's my husband...*kept repeating in my head. I had no doubt that he was my one true love, and no promises or Bible verses mattered at that point.

However, over the years, I'd begun to regret not having the memories of a full-blown wedding to accompany the man of my dreams. I wanted to walk down an aisle to him. I wanted to have "our song" played. I wanted a white dress. I wanted wedding photos. So where's the easiest place to do this? Las Vegas.

An Entertaining Way to Cope

We didn't want extravagance. It would still be just the four of us there. We booked a little wedding chapel online that looked like an indoor garden. I reveled in taking my daughter with me to buy a wedding dress. It was simple, yet classy and elegant, and flattered my older-bride figure. We also found a cute bridesmaid dress for my daughter, as well as a shirt and tie for my son. I'd practically fallen in love with my husband the moment he played a Yanni song for me, so I wanted to make sure to walk down the aisle to that song. Our package came with a photographer, videographer, clergy, and flowers. I was so excited to renew our vows!

During the week leading up to our departure, I had a strange pain around my ribcage. It came and went. It was like a cramp around my lungs and it made it difficult to take a deep breath. I just figured I'd pulled a muscle or something and put it aside.

As we were going through airport security, it started cramping again. I tried stretching and twisting but nothing helped. We were waiting at our gate to board, and I was quite uncomfortable. I needed to take a deep breath but I couldn't. We walked down the jetway to board the plane and I kept trying to shake it off. We found our seats and once I sat down, it grew worse. It was as though I had a squeezing band around my ribcage. I decided to stand in the back while people boarded. The flight attendant asked me what was wrong and chalked it up to anxiety. I explained that I had never had a fear of flying. I'd flown countless times without a problem. She had me breathe in through my nose and out through my mouth. It didn't help. I tried to convince myself that I was fine and went back to my seat. A lady seated near me heard me complaining to my husband, and shared with me an all-natural, chewable anti-anxiety pill. I popped it in my mouth and tried to get comfortable. Suddenly, the plane started to slowly roll backward and I freaked!

Oh my gosh! What is wrong with me?! What if I get up in the air and I can't breathe? Why do I have this pain in my chest? I can't do this, I can't do this!!!

I jumped up and hit the flight attendant's button above my seat. My husband was trying to calm me down. This was not like me. I'm one of those calm and rational people who annoyingly follows all rules and never draws attention to myself.

The flight attendant made it to my seat and I blurted, "I can't do this!!"

Although she was understandably put-off, she tried to smile and said, "Would you like to get off the plane?"

I didn't hesitate, "Yes!"

The plane stopped moving. I gathered my carry-on items and told my family to go ahead without me. They argued, but I was insistent.

"Just go. I'll be fine. I'll figure out a way to get to you." The three of them stared up at me.

Then, the pilot got on the speaker system, "Ladies and Gentlemen, we're sorry but a passenger needs to exit the plane. We will be pulling back up to the gate. This will cause a delay. We apologize for the inconvenience."

An Entertaining Way to Cope

Of course, we were sitting at the back of the plane.
People were grumbling and looking around to see who the
troublemaker was. I stood up and began walking down
the narrow, forever-long, aisle as everyone on the plane
watched my walk of shame.

*Oh my gosh. This is humiliating. Everyone is staring at
me. They all hate me. This is the longest aisle on any
plane ever in history. Yes, sir. I'm the one causing the
problem. Thank you for your dirty look. I appreciate it.*

When I got to the front, I instinctually apologized to every
airline employee. I hated being a nuisance. I walked
through the tunnel and back into the gate area, tears
streaming down my face.

The airline employees somewhat tried to comfort me,
but they had a job to do. Apparently it's a big deal for
someone to ask to get off of an airplane but to leave their
checked bag on it. I tried to convince them that my
family, who was still on the plane, would pick it up at the
baggage claim in Las Vegas. It didn't occur to me that
this situation is a big no-no and that policy states they
must prevent a possible terrorist situation by locating and
removing my suitcase.

I felt awful for causing this delay, so I finally said, "I
understand why you need to take that precaution, but if
my bag contained something deadly, do you think I would
have left my husband and two children on the flight?"

I guess the authority above them decided I made a good
point, and they decided not to delay the flight any further.

My husband and children were texting me nonstop.

This was not how our family vacation was supposed to start. They were worried about me. My husband was also laughing at me because I was the cause of the airline sending him a text notifying him that his flight was delayed. I convinced them that I would be fine.

I sat in the empty terminal trying to determine what to do next. After the plane once again backed away and headed for the runway, the airline employee asked me what I wanted to do.

In tears, I explained, "My wedding dress is on that plane! My husband and I are supposed to renew our wedding vows at a ceremony in two days. I have to figure out a way to get there. I'm not afraid to fly. I'm having a medical issue and I don't know what's going on."

I think the words *wedding dress* are what got them. After a few clicks on her computer, she found a flight for me the next morning and didn't charge me a cent. I just needed to get home and figure out what was wrong with me.

I called my doctor's office and hysterically blabbed all about my situation with too-detailed descriptions of my pain, my walk of shame and my upcoming wedding. They were able to get me in that afternoon. They checked my heart and lungs and all seemed to be fine. I was comforted to be able to rule out an impending heart attack, despite what my panic-stricken brain told me. I still didn't understand why I had this clinching pain that would come and go around my ribs. My doctor decided it was anxiety and wrote a prescription.

I'd never struggled with anxiety before. I didn't even know the symptoms. But hearing that I was physically okay was enough to help me feel comfortable flying the next day.

The pain around my ribcage came and went throughout the night. *How is it anxiety if I'm asleep?* When it was time to wake up, the pain was still there so I took one of the anti-anxiety pills. After an hour, I felt sleepy and loopy but still unable to take a deep breath. I called my doctor to ask how often I could take the pills. I was still afraid to get on the flight not being able to breathe, but if an anti-anxiety pill could get me to Las Vegas, I'd do it.

She told me I could take one every eight hours. By the time I'd board the plane, it would have been six hours. I didn't want it to wear off during the flight, so I decided to take another one once I arrived at the gate.

I don't remember that flight at all. Apparently I'd consumed a couple bags of chips and pretzels and even watched a movie. I know I was awake and could even talk, but I was not aware of it. I began to become a little more lucid as we were about to land in Las Vegas. The man sitting next to me asked, "Are you okay?"

"Yes, why?" I asked.

He said, "You just don't seem okay."

I was still fully clothed so I wondered what I had said or done to cause concern. It didn't matter. I'd made it to Vegas. I somehow floated out to get a taxi. I don't remember telling the driver where to take me, but I must have. On the drive there, he suddenly swerved the car left then right, all while cussing and honking. It seems that our street crossed over an airport runway and a plane was making a late ascent. The driver thought the plane was about to hit us.

He cussed and shouted, "Do you see that friggin' plane?! It nearly ran into us! Oh my gosh!"

However, I was in loopy la-la land, not a care in the world.

Plane? What plane?

I arrived at our resort and was greeted by my very happy, relieved family. They had no idea I was dosed up on anti-anxiety medication so when my husband promptly handed me a strawberry daiquiri to enjoy poolside, I accepted.

And passed out on a pool chair.

A couple of days later, I had the wedding of my dreams. Everything was perfect, from the music, to the vows, to the flowers, to my husband's teary eyes. I have the pictures to prove it.

Later, my daughter confessed that she'd been terrified on that flight without me. She thought I'd had some sixth sense intuition about the plane crashing and that's why I'd gotten off. I sarcastically responded to her, "Yeah, right. Like I'd say, "Uh, I have a feeling the plane is going to crash so I'm getting off but y'all stay here..."

It wasn't until the following year that I was diagnosed with MS. As I had no clue what it was or what symptoms it caused, I hadn't realized that Missy had been the cause of my walk of shame down the airplane aisle. Apparently Missy loves to give hugs, also known as MS hugs. The squeezing around my ribcage was one of Missy's first introductions but I hadn't known her. Still to this day, she enjoys squeezing me affectionately and even though I've tried to tell her I'm not that kind of girl, she does it anyway.

Tunnel of Doom

I've had an MRI before. Of my knee. I remember having to lie still and hear all of the banging. Of course, only my legs were in the machine, so when I was told I needed to get an MRI of my brain and spine, I wasn't concerned at all.

I'd learned to face medical issues with a smile and an overabundance of confidence. I changed into the gown and lightheartedly climbed on the table.

Wait, hold up! You're putting a cage over my face?! And stuffing the sides with cloths so I can't move at all? Uh, is my nose going to clear the ceiling of this tunnel? I swear my eyelashes are brushing the top of this tube. Does air even get in here? This must be what a coffin would feel like. I don't want to be in a coffin dead; I certainly don't want to be in one alive. I'm not that big yet my shoulders and elbows are squished in here! How long will I have to be like this?!

"Are you doing okay, Janelle?"

"Yep!" I lied.

The banging and thumping began. I tried to get my mind off of being squeezed into a test tube by trying to make a little song out of the rhythmic banging. I tried to focus on the beat.

Boom, rattle rattle rattle, boom.

Gosh, it's hot in here. There's no way I'm getting enough air to breathe. Don't freak out, Janelle. You're ridiculous. You can do this.

But I want out of this thing! Where's the little button they said I could squeeze in an emergency? This is a frickin' emergency and I can't find the dumb button! I'm gonna die.

The banging paused and switched into another rhythm. I was sweating. I could no longer breathe through my nose. I breathed through my mouth instead. I tried so hard to be good.

"Janelle, I need you to not swallow. We'll have to redo that image."

Okay, I'm flat on my back with my head held down with a brace and now I can't swallow? Don't swallow. Don't swallow. But the back of my throat is filling up with spit. Don't swallow. But I need to swallow. How come I never notice the need to swallow except when I'm told not to? Crap, I'm about to swallow. I don't want to have them redo it again. I want out of here. I don't dare choke on my spit because I can't sit up to cough. Can I drown in my own saliva?

Finally the blessed pause between banging rhythms. I hoped it was safe to swallow. I sneaked it in and they don't say anything.

I should have asked how long this was going to take. Maybe I could count the seconds, total them into minutes and figure out how much longer I have to go.

I counted to sixty so many times and there wasn't an end in sight. My body ached from being so still. It was stuffy and warm. Suddenly, the sounds stopped and I could hear the man come into the room; my body started to slide out of the tube.

An Entertaining Way to Cope

Yay! I made it! I survived. It's over.

"I need you to not move at all. I'm going to inject this dye in your arm," he said.

Are you kidding me?!

Being cooperative, "Okay. How much longer do we have?"

"We're about halfway finished."

Good Lord, take me now. I can't do this anymore. Even a corpse doesn't stay still this long. They're putting me back into this mouse hole. I swear I'm breathing in my own carbon dioxide. I am never doing this again. I'm trapped. Do tears rolling down my face count as movement? I can imagine him saying, "Janelle, I need you to stop crying as the speed of your tears is blurring the image."

I tried everything I could think of. I tried to remember words to songs. I tried focusing and relaxing each little part of my body. I tried to decide what I was going to eat as a reward if I survived this. I tried naming every animal I could think of. I tried praying.

Finally, the noises stopped and I heard the door open. My body began its glorious course to freedom.

"You're all finished!" he joyfully exclaimed as if I'd completed an exciting race.

I was sweaty, exhausted and traumatized. I stared at him and stumbled out of the room. I'd been in that coffin for two hours, ten hours postmortem time.

No dessert or amount of alcohol would be a worthy reward for enduring that hell.

Of course, that experience revealed my relationship with Missy. She showed her presence as significant lesions on my brain. Much to my horror, having Missy meant having MRIs several times a year.

Oh hell to the no.

It took me a few panic-filled episodes before I created my particular MRI Recipe for Success.

1. Instead of their scratchy hospital gowns, wear my own clothes consisting of yoga pants, a t-shirt and a sports bra with no metal clips.
2. Refuse the blanket.
3. Make two things very clear to the radiology tech:
    a. If I squeeze that help button, he/she has 15 seconds to get me out after which there will be **no** discussion, persuasion or attempted comforting. (With this clear, I no longer feel trapped and have never needed to squeeze the button.)
    b. (S)he will tell me the duration of each upcoming image. This lets me know when we're between images and I can blink, wiggle my nose and swallow. It also breaks the two hours into manageable 3 to 5 minute increments, which are easier to get through. (One guy told me he didn't have time to do that. I asked him if he had time to clean up urine or vomit in the tunnel. My point was made and he cooperated.)
4. Select a facility that offers headphones with music

and/or goggles with changing images or at the very least puts a wash cloth over the head brace to prevent feeling or seeing the ceiling that is looming a half-inch above my face.

5. Take an anti-anxiety medication. I rarely use these but I'd rather feel loopy and sleepy in that tube than like a trapped lioness who's about to chew off her own skin.

6. Schedule the MRI in December whenever possible. Listening to Christmas music made for the happiest, jolliest two hours ever spent in that machine. Who could be frightened while listening to Jolly Old St. Nicholas or mentally singing along to Rudolph?

7. Wear a soothing scent or essential oil. Instead of worrying that I was inhaling the same stale molecules of air over and over, I breathe in a scent that makes me happy and content. (A radiology tech once walked in after my test was complete and said, "Compared to how people usually smell after being in there, I'd take the way you smell every time!" I guess people sweating and peeing on themselves from fear doesn't smell very good. Take a hint, sir!)

So thanks to Missy, I get the pleasure of frequent MRIs. Missy considers them her quarterly photo shoot. She loves seeing herself on the images and always seems quite proud of her appearance.

Magic Mike Baby!

I had been teaching all day. I was finally home, wobbling in on numb, exhausted legs. This was no longer unusual, just a fact of my life. Before my diagnosis, I thought the muscle pain I felt every night was just part of getting older! I laid down on the couch to rest and to watch television. Fortunately, my kids had already eaten and were doing homework. Suddenly, I noticed something flashing from the edge of my peripheral vision. Over the next few minutes, the flashing spread toward the center of my vision and turned to darkness. Remember, I only see out of one eye, so I couldn't see much at all at this point. I remained calm and called for my daughter to come upstairs. I asked her to research what was happening to me on her smart phone. I was definitely getting the impression that I should go to an emergency room. Fortunately, my husband then came in from work. I calmly told him what was going on and that I needed to go to the emergency room, only five minutes away. We got in the car and began down roads that I've traveled regularly for over eight years. But for some reason, I didn't recognize where I was. My vision was still hindered, but even what I could see from the windows wasn't familiar.

I told my husband, "I don't know where we are."

Thinking it was only due to my vision, he comforted me saying, "It's okay, Honey. We'll be there in a little bit."

Growing more frantic, I said again, "No, really. I do not know where we are."

Then it hit me and I started to panic, "I don't know who YOU are!!"

I knew that I should know him and that he was a safe person but that's all I knew. I had no idea what his name was.

As I had made perfect sense mere seconds before, he thought I was just joking and he confidently shouted out, "Well, I'm Magic Mike, Baby!"

What's funny is that I didn't know who my husband was but I seemed to sense he wasn't "Magic Mike."

Then, I was screaming, "I'm serious! I don't know who you are!!"

With his strip-teasing dancer dream busted, he suddenly realized I was serious. He patted my leg and said, "I'm Greg, Baby. It's okay."

Once I heard his name, I recognized it as correct and settled down a little bit.

We walked into the emergency room triage area. My husband filled out the form explaining our medical need. I sat in the waiting room, terrified. I began to panic again. I couldn't see much and I didn't recognize the part I *could* see. Suddenly, I felt very hot and faint. I started taking off my shirt and yelling, "HELP!"

The other people in the waiting area were staring at me and the room was eerily quiet. As I said, I am usually a quiet person: I follow rules, act respectfully, and do not cause a fuss. This was *not* like me at all.

However, note to self, screaming and stripping in a waiting room *does* make one skip the line and receive both immediate assistance and a private room. Ha! They questioned me about my symptoms. I was throwing them for a loop; they obviously weren't used to someone coming in with vision loss, one eye already blind and memory loss.

I tried to tell them what I could and couldn't see. I could see the right edge of my nose and maybe a centimeter from there. Everything else was gone. Not dark or black. Gone. Apparently, when I tried to explain the bit of vision I *could* see, it didn't make sense to people with vision in both eyes who have studied about fully-visioned patients.

They asked me basic questions to check for mental status.

"What year is it?"

I know I know this. How ridiculous of me that I can't remember the year. Two thousand something. Good grief! Why don't I know the year?

I couldn't even get the words *two thousand* out of my mouth before he said, "It's okay. Who's the President?"

Uh, uh, uh. Oh my gosh. Why don't I know this stuff?

"Bush?" I weakly guessed. A girl could dream I suppose.

The answer was Obama. Once I was told the answer, I recognized it as correct.

"What month is it?" he asked.

Again, I know I know this. What an easy question. What the heck? I'll take a guess.

"August?" I hoped. *Jeopardy here I come.*

"It's December," he answered and scribbled down a note. *Altered mental status*, I would later discover.

I kept begging my husband to keep asking me questions. I wanted to know what I *didn't* know.

"When are the kids' birthdays?" he asked.

Thankfully I seemed to remember that I *had* kids and didn't respond with, "What kids?" I couldn't, however, remember their birthdays.

The phrase "drawing a blank" had new meaning to me at this point. That's literally what my mind felt like. He'd ask me a question and...*nothing.* No answer came to my mind. Things I knew I should know. I just stared at him until he gave me the answers and it would click in my brain as, *"Oh yeah. That's right."*

He continued on with question after question. "What's the name of the school where you teach?" "What's the principal's name?"

I knew I knew these answers, but I couldn't recall them.

Think of how it feels when a website asks for your username and password. There's that blank, "Oh, crap," and then panic. But multiply that feeling by 100.

Eventually, the ER staff took note of my MS diagnosis and consulted a neurologist. He confirmed that my symptoms seemed like a MS flare and ordered hospitalization.

The emergency room was a stand alone building several miles away from the hospital, so this meant I'd have my first ambulance ride.

I still could hardly see, so my other senses of touch and sound were hyper-aware.

I was strapped tightly to a stretcher and wheeled out of the building. I listened for any groans of exertion when it came to hoisting me into the ambulance and was relieved that they didn't let any out. I can imagine the training manual for first responders: *Under no circumstances should you grunt or groan when lifting a patient into the vehicle. To do so would be rude.*

A lady I couldn't see introduced herself and explained that she'd be riding alongside me.

As the ride began, I started to question exactly what kind of vehicle they had me in. I'd ridden in the backs of pick-up trucks back in the good ol' days when kids were allowed to do this. I'd bounced along in a ski boat over white-capped waves. I'd had wild rides on the back of a 4-wheeler as it zoomed over bumps and hills. Roll all of these experiences into one and add to that the image of being inside a toaster that rattles, rumbles, and creaks, like it's going to collapse at any second…that's what this ambulance ride was like.

At the hospital, I was promptly given two hours of lovely MRIs. Unlike most of my MRI experiences in which I required anti-anxiety medication, relaxation techniques and a series of promises made by the tech, I slept through this one like a baby. Apparently the fear of going blind and losing one's memory is exhausting.

An Entertaining Way to Cope

The MRIs showed I had new and enhancing lesions in the areas of my brain affecting vision and memory. After a few days in the hospital receiving IV steroids, my vision, although blurred, returned.

As for my memory, I'd actually lost my "recall," not my memory. That's why, once Greg reminded me that his name was Greg, I recognized it as correct. I'd blanked out much of the past ten years. Once I was reminded of something, I could recall it. It took several weeks to refill all of those holes.

Living with Missy means I have to laugh at difficult things sometimes. This episode, although rare according to my doctor, has given my family and me material to joke with ever since. I conveniently "forget" my kids' names when they're on my last nerve. *"What's your name again?"*

As for my husband, I think he needs a diagnosis. I swear he actually believes he's Magic Mike.

And the Eyes Have It

As I had vision only in the right eye, due to childhood blindness, we didn't mess around when it came to protecting my eyesight. I'd temporarily and sporadically lost vision several times in my good eye because Missy placed a lesion on my occipital lobe. Therefore, my doctor ordered all vision tests possible to make sure we didn't miss anything.

Missy has a sick sense of humor. She could attack any part of my brain that she chose. She particularly selected my left occipital lobe, which affects the vision in my right eye. Had she chosen to attack the other occipital lobe, it wouldn't have mattered because I already didn't have vision in my left eye. She's such a b-b-witch.

I can't compare my vision loss to that of other MS sufferers, most of who see with both eyes. My warning that I'm about to lose my vision is a flashing light in my peripheral vision. That flashing spreads to my central vision in a matter of minutes. I can hold my hand in front of my face and not see it. I can usually see a bit from the side of my nose and over just a bit. Everything else disappears. It's not "black" like when you close your eyes. It's just missing, if that makes sense. It usually lasts anywhere from a few minutes to several hours. Fortunately, my vision always returns. What happens to me is often compared to an ocular migraine, but as I have a MS lesion on my occipital lobe, doctors deduce that is the cause.

Not being able to see is my worst nightmare. Literally. Since I was a child, I've had countless dreams that I was blind. In those dreams, I try everything to "open my eyes" so I can see but nothing works. I use my other senses to try to compensate. I wake up terrified, yet relieved that I can see.

We made the hour-long drive for a vision field test to a hospital that had state-of-the-art equipment. My husband stayed in the waiting room while I was taken back to a dim room. The lady introduced herself and explained what the test would entail. She attached electrodes to my head that would signal my brain activity, revealing what my eyes could see.

"I'll have you cover one eye and you'll watch the screen with the other eye," she began her rote speech.

I interrupted, "I have vision only in one eye. My right eye."

I guess this wasn't an unusual response because she immediately replied, "Well, I'll still have you try."

I'm assuming people who take this test consider themselves blind or unable to see out of one or both eyes, but *do* see, just not well. I do not fit into this category of people.

I said, "No, you don't understand. I'm blind in my left eye. It's actually a prosthetic eye."

This made her pause for a moment. She then said, "Well, I'll still have you follow the way the test is designed, one eye at a time."

The always complacent, do-what-I'm-told me said, "Okay. I'll do whatever you want, but I'm telling you that I can't see out of my prosthetic eye."

The always encouraging, do-what-I-say lady said, "You just might be surprised what that eye sees!"

Hell, yeah, I would be. If a piece of ceramic in my eye socket actually has the ability to produce vision, it would be a worldwide miracle. It occurred to me to explain this to her.

"Do you understand that I have a prosthetic eye? It's a piece of ceramic," I said.

Continuing to adjust her machine and put on the electrodes, she happily said, "It's amazing what prosthetics can do these days."

What? Are you kidding me?

I tried again, "Well, I know that prosthetic legs help people walk and prosthetic arms help people pick up and carry things, but prosthetic eyes do **not** help people see."

She looked at me for a second and said, "Really?"

Oh. My. Gosh. How do you qualify for this job?

In frustration, I took off my glasses, looked straight at her, and with my pretty pink acrylic fingernail, I tap-tap-tapped on my prosthetic eye.

And stared at her.

I'd never done that to anyone before. I always try to hide the fact that I have a prosthetic eye. I go to highly-trained professionals to make my eye look as close to my other eye as possible. Many people who've known me for years don't know it's a prosthetic. My own husband and children have never seen me without my eye. I certainly don't draw attention to it.

But this lady was on my last nerve.

"See?" I tap-tap-tapped it again, "It's not real. I can't see out of it."

She finally seemed a bit taken aback and admitted, "I don't know how to run the test on only one eye."

I can understand that. "Okay, do what you have to do."

She began, "Cover your right eye and stare at the screen."

Feeling so stupid, I covered the eye I can see out of and stared straight ahead assuming that my piece of ceramic was pointed in the direction of the screen. Obviously, I had no idea what was happening on that screen.

Continuing her daily rote speech she said, "You're doing good."

I reiterated, "You do know that I can't see anything on there, right?" as I continued to keep my good eye covered.

"Well according to your brain waves, you're seeing something!" she happily reported.

What the f---?!

At this point I was tempted to pop out my piece of ceramic and lay it on the table in front of me and ask her to continue running the test and let me know what that eye is "seeing."

But I decided that was a bit much.

I suggested, "Could it be that my brain waves are reacting to my *right* eye staring at the palm of my hand as it's covering up my eye?"

"No," she adamantly stated, "not unless those brain waves have learned to read the other side of your brain."

I patiently educated her, "Well, because I lost vision in that eye at a young age, I've been told that my brain has compensated for that in many ways. Maybe that's what you're seeing."

She didn't respond and instead instructed, "Okay, now cover your left eye."

Really? Really. Okay, I will hold my hand up and cover the piece of ceramic to stop it from "seeing" anything.

Images of my prosthetic eye lying on a table in front of me reappeared in my mind. I pictured myself reaching out to the table and covering up my "eye" for this test. I chuckled.

I was past the point of humiliation and frustration. This woman's stupidity had become my daily dose of amusement. I began giggling. Giggling causes my head to jiggle.

"I need you to be still," she commanded.

Oh crap. Nothing triggers a fit of laughter more than being told I'm not allowed to laugh. It used to happen in church all the time. I was supposed to be quiet and solemn but something would happen that would set off a round of giggles. Trying to hold it in only made it worse. Bouncing silently, hiding the smile, while holding my breath and trying to suppress my laughter would backfire. Little bursts of air and voice would pop out from my lips, drawing attention to my fit of laughter. I'd instantly be reprimanded by my parents and the humor would disappear. Temporarily. Golly, if I could total up the amount of time I passed in church trying not to laugh...

I took a few breaths and tried to relax and get my mind off of this hilarious situation. I obediently stared at the screen in front of me, with a big, unexplained smile on my face. Every once in a while, a giggle from the absurdity would escape from my lips. The screen was flashing and blipping and changing colors. I couldn't tell what I was supposed to be looking at, but apparently whatever my eye was seeing was telling my brain about it. I decided this is as close to being "high" as I was ever going to feel. I laughed uncontrollably as I stared at flashing lights, while covering up an imaginary eye.

After a while, the vision test came to an end. As much as I'd tried to hide my laughter, the lady probably figured out I was actually laughing *at her,* so she was rather subdued and businesslike at this point. She removed the electrodes from my head and led me back to the waiting room.

I walked in and announced to my husband, "Good news! I can see out of my left eye!" which brought on a very confused expression.

I questioned the validity of the test results, which stated that I had limited vision in my left eye, even though it noted that the left eye was prosthetic. The good news was that the eye I could actually see out of only had minimal damage.

If it weren't for Missy, I'd never have this funny story to tell.

A Silver Lining

A severe lesion caused me to lose feeling on the entire left side of my body, from my scalp to my toes. Missy covered my body with a thin layer of cloth. I couldn't feel light touch, textures, or temperatures. For some people, these feelings return after steroids and time, but it didn't for me. Missy was pleased for causing this permanent damage; she enjoyed playing games with it.

I am right handed but I never realized how much I rely on my left hand. When I am shopping for clothing, I reach out to feel the fabric with my left hand. Every. Single. Time. Even years later. And each time, Missy reminds me, "Uh, you can't feel that, can you," and she snickers as I am forced to use my right hand instead.

My clothes dryer buzzes. Since I am a wife and mother, I have completed a trillion loads of laundry by this point and could do it in my sleep. I open the door and reach in with my *left* hand to test if the clothes are dry. I do this with my left hand. Every. Single. Time. Missy laughs because she knows I can't feel the difference between wet and dry; trying is useless. I sigh and reach in with my right hand to see if more drying time is needed. This is one more reminder that Missy is my constant companion, and she has a sick sense of humor.

Missy loves when we shower. I turn on the shower and inevitably reach in with my *left* hand to test the water temperature before stepping in. It feels fine because I don't realize I can't feel it. I step in with my left foot. It still feels fine because I can't actually feel the temperature! I step in with my right foot and wham! The scalding hot water registers in my brain and I jump out of the way. Missy laughs and reminds me how stupid I am and how she'll always be here to remind me. I've lost count how many times she has played this particular trick on me. I wish I'd wise up to it, but I blame her for that as well.

I have to consciously remind myself, every single time, to reach out with my *right* hand instead. It's the times like these that healthy people take for granted. People underestimate the brainpower required for people with neurological illnesses to complete simple tasks. Breathing and blinking are things our bodies do automatically, without having to think about it. Reaching to touch something *becomes* automatic after having done it repeatedly. The same goes for walking. Our legs lift, move and step without us having to consciously tell them. Unless Missy is involved. These simple activities require as much thought, concentration and memory as completing a complex algebra equation.

For example: Doing Laundry. The clothes dryer goes off. *Buzz!* I slowly stand.

Am I balanced? Is my left foot touching the floor? Okay, leg: lift, stretch out, foot on the floor. Keep my balance. Step with my other leg. Shift my body weight. Repeat.

This is the internal dialogue required for merely walking. Heaven forbid someone chooses that moment to shout, "Mom?! Where are my soccer cleats?" My brain shifts over to that line of thought and forgets to keep telling my legs how to walk and *bam!* I'm suddenly face first on the floor.

I eventually arrive at the dryer and automatically open it with my stronger right hand. My left hand begins to reach...*stop!* I make my right hand reach in to feel if the clothes are still wet or dry.

An Entertaining Way to Cope

This is a one-minute example of my brain activity on a normal day. Imagine what it's like to require that much concentration hour after hour every single day. No wonder Missy causes extreme fatigue. Maybe healthy people could get the idea if they try to solve that complex algebra equation while someone nearby bangs pots together and someone else sticks fingers in and out of that person's ears. Add in the internal dialogue of Missy reminding them how tired, achy and stupid they are. Yeah. That might come close to understanding it. Go ahead. Solve the algebra problem now.

However, as miserable as Missy makes me, I am determined to find the silver lining her rain cloud over me causes.

I no longer get cold easily because half of my body can't feel the temperature anyway! Restaurant air conditioners used to drive me crazy. Now I can comfortably enjoy my meal because I can't feel the cold air blowing on me.

I went a whole day with a hole in my sock. At the end of the day, I took off my shoes and noticed my big toe sticking all the way out of the end of the sock. I hadn't felt it!

That tag on the inside of my jeans that scratches and rubs all day? It doesn't bother me anymore.

Mosquito bites? I don't feel them land, bite, or itch.

(My husband wishes that I "can't feel" him sneaking feels of certain body parts, but I can *see* him so that ruins his plan.)

Hey, we have to focus on the good things, people. Missy is determined to make me miserable. One of my forms of survival is to take her power of negativity away from her.

Laughing at Myself

I was a straight-A student. I was even labeled "gifted." I had a great memory, was a strong reader, and was quick at math. I graduated at the top of my class in high school and with honors from college.

So why the heck can I not remember what I'm supposed to do with that knob-thingy in the shower? I stare at it. I know I'm finished with my shower, and I know I'm supposed to do something with that knob, but for the life of me, I can't remember what it is.

Do I turn it? Pull it up? Push it down?

I know I know the answer because I've been showering in the same shower for 10 years.

The water continues to pour down on me while I stare at the knob. I reach out and touch it. I turn it to the left and the water becomes very hot. I jump out of the way and decide to try again. I reach around the hot water for the knob and try lifting it up. It doesn't lift, nor does it push down.

Why can't I remember something as simple as how to turn the shower off? I eventually twist the knob all the way to the right and the water shuts off.

Talk about feeling stupid! I grew up with the reputation of being smart. I *am* smart. I know I'm smart. But Missy certainly makes me feel stupid.

Another time, I'm rushing out the door to pick my son up from basketball practice. I grab my purse, go out the door, close it and get in the car.

Silence. Stillness. Now what do I do? I can't figure out what to do next in this daily activity of "taxi-ing" my kids. I look around the quiet car. I know I'm supposed to do something, but I can't remember what it is. I think I need something. *What do I need?* Suddenly, I notice my purse sitting in the other seat. *Oh yeah! Keys! I need my keys to start the car.* I dig through my purse, past the piles of receipts, and I find the keys. I can start on my way.

Except it would help if I was sitting in the *driver's* seat instead of the passenger's seat. What, do I think I'm in England?!

I could easily cry about my situation. It would make sense to feel sorry for myself. I could get angry. It's so unfair to have to live like this. How degrading for me to fall from the top of my class, to being unable to manage even the simplest of tasks.

But what do I do? I laugh. I laugh and laugh and laugh. At myself. *Wait until people hear this story! I'm supposed to be getting into the car to pick up my son. Instead I'm sitting in the* passenger *seat of an otherwise empty car and can't figure out what I'm supposed to do next! How ridiculous!*

Darn Missy. She has a wicked sense of humor.

Fix It and Forget It

"Janelle, how do you stay so positive?" This is probably the question I am asked the most. Then they report how miserable they'd be if they had to live the way I do.

It made me stop and think. How *do* I stay so positive? A lot of it is natural, I suppose. I've had several past health problems yet I've never experienced it as misery, much less wallowed in it. I preferred to compensate and move on with my life. However, Missy doesn't play fair. She doesn't *let* me compensate and move on. So how do I do it?

I grew up with a chronically-ill mother. She was in and out of hospitals my entire life. She struggled with severe asthma; the steroids that helped her breathe wreaked havoc on her body. She had thin skin that tore easily. Osteoporosis made her toes curl and cross, making walking a struggle for her. She was prone to infections. But, guess what? She didn't complain. She smiled. She laughed. She tackled every obstacle. And heaven forbid she ever went to an emergency room without the laundry done and her make-up on. So, the standard she set as my role model was pretty high. Although she passed away seven years before my MS diagnosis, her positive attitude was engrained in me.

Another way I manage to stay positive? It takes too much darn energy to be negative! This is something I never would have realized without having MS. Healthy people take their energy levels for granted. Of course it takes energy to exercise and to go to work. But do they realize how much energy it takes to sit on a couch? I'll bet they don't, because I didn't either until I developed MS. Holding my arm in a resting position on my stomach requires energy. Keeping my head upright takes energy. I had to learn to change the way I *sit* (usually sitting in itself *is* resting) in order to rest my body. I put my head back and flop my arms to my sides. I evaluate whether I am unwittingly using any of my muscles. Only once I have completely relaxed every muscle can I actually rest.

Do you realize how much energy emotions use? People think of energy as it pertains to physical activity. But there's a reason getting angry causes our heart rate to elevate. Adrenaline causes our bodies to get fired up which uses a lot of energy!

I've learned to let things go more quickly and more easily. When my son leaves his wet towel on the carpet, does it frustrate me? You bet! I snap at him to fix it, give him a piece of my mind and promptly move on. Dropped. Done.

The old me would have stayed angry about it. I would have stomped off muttering to myself and hastily sought out other messes. I would have used that angry energy to have a rant session in my head:

"Can you believe this?! I work hard to wash and dry the towels so they don't get mildewed and he leaves towels wet on the floor? I've told him a thousand times to hang up his towel! I quit. Everyone in the house can just rub the smell of mildewed towels on their clean after-showered bodies. Or better yet, they can air dry in the nude. Nobody appreciates the things I do around here. I'm so sick and tired of cleaning up after everyone..."

Hours later, when he'd come out from hiding, I'd take one look at him and likely snap at him again.

Now? Who has the energy for that crap?! It's a wet towel! Fix it and forget it. Maybe my memory issues are a blessing in disguise because I literally can't remember what I was mad about, or even *that* I was mad, 30 seconds later.

Holding a grudge? Never! It takes too much energy to remain at that high level of anger, remember the reason for the anger and to figure out passive-aggressive ways to punish the perpetrator.

Unfortunately, my husband hasn't learned this lesson. Let's say I merely suggest a slight correction to his motor vehicle operation. This is a pet peeve of his and one area I know better than to step into. But I open my mouth and calmly suggest that he slow down a bit and stay in his own lane, (while gasping, jerking and grabbing onto a handle) and before I can blink, he's mad. *I've done it again.* He'll loudly erupt and go on a rant for several minutes. I'll regret saying anything for the umpteenth time.

Literally seconds later, I've forgotten the whole episode. I'm back to being content and easy-going. I'll begin to talk about whatever is next on my mind and happily carry on a one-sided conversation without even noticing it's one-sided. I'll add humor to my stories and laugh and laugh. Maybe an hour later, (*several* hours later?) I'll notice that he's quiet and I'll ask why. To my shock, he'll let me know how mad he still is about my telling him how to drive!

Wait. What? But that was so long ago! I'd forgotten all about it.

That's when it occurred to me how much energy it takes to be angry. I learned to quickly let go of the issue and negative emotions. It takes much less energy to be happy. I remember looking at my husband in that moment and saying, "You don't know how lucky you are to have enough energy to stay upset about something for so long."

But truly I think I'm the lucky one. It's okay, Missy. Take the energy needed for anger. I'd rather put it into being happy. I'm happy most of the time now. It's all I have energy for. People see me as being positive all the time. Okay. I'll accept that.

Remission. What's That?

I was diagnosed with Relapsing Remitting Multiple Sclerosis. This is what most people with MS are diagnosed with. Let's focus on the word Remitting.

When we hear that someone's cancer is in remission, it brings joy and relief! It means the cancer is no longer active and they can resume a healthy life. That's what I expected with RRMS.

I'm a dork who loves to research. Google is a good friend of mine. I select topics and read article after article to educate myself. I don't believe every word I read, so whatever is mentioned the most often is what I'll walk away with as reasonable fact.

I'd exhausted my research on RRMS, and I was relieved to learn that people have phases of remission.

Yay! I can become healthy again! Full of energy? Awesome! Can't wait. I'm waiting....and waiting...and waiting. Several years later, I'm wondering, "Where in the heck is my remission?" I still can't feel anything on the left side of my body. My vision comes and goes. I'm forgetful.

My research explains that damage done to the body by brain lesions won't necessarily go back to normal. But what about the other MS symptoms? I've been living with fatigue for years. I can't go through an entire day without practicing the head back, arms down routine of resting at least a few times. If I get too warm, the left side of my body cramps and I slur my words. Doesn't remission mean that this disease will go away for a while? When is that going to happen? I'm waiting.

Ha-ha! I blinked and missed it. Apparently in my case, in the ten years before I was diagnosed, I *did* have remissions. All those times I had weird symptoms but they'd go away and I'd move on with my life? Yep. Remissions. But by the time I was finally diagnosed, the disease had progressed to a phase where my body was irreparably damaged and supposed remission isn't actually noticeable.

Remission for me still consists of fatigue, numbness, spasticity, vision loss and memory loss. It's my baseline. I can't feel better, only worse.

I do continue to have flare-ups and some new symptoms. My doctor has suggested, unofficially, that I might have Primary Progressive MS (PPMS). In my opinion, the name and classification does not matter. I have MS. I have it every day. Missy no longer takes vacations without me. Nor do I get any vacations without her. She is by my side every minute of every day. If nothing else, she's loyal.

MS Walk

"Mom, I'd like to put together a team for our local MS walk. Is that okay?" announced my 15-year-old daughter. I say "announced" instead of "asked," because teenagers have a way of announcing they're doing something, rather than actually asking.

I was a bit surprised because being involved in a "cause" and taking on a leadership role, weren't typical of her. But I wasn't going to stop her.

It hadn't been long since I'd been diagnosed, so the MS walk was something I'd never heard of nor experienced. I wasn't sure what was involved.

With a confidence beyond her years she said, "Don't worry, Mom. I've got it," and she did. She started our team, publicized it, got donations and added more team members. Before I knew it, "Janelle's Journey" was a growing, active team.

We decided our team would wear green, my favorite color. Also, I had a green shirt that said "MS Sucks" in huge letters and I wanted to wear it. Everyone was given green bandanas to signify membership in our group. Many dear friends of mine arrived that morning to walk in my honor.

How humbling. I sheepishly admitted to myself that never had I participated in an event like this, for any cause or any person I knew. What a shame that it took Missy entering my life for me to receive a lesson on humility.

As everyone gathered and prepared to walk around our city's river walk, the irony hit me. Why is there an MS

Walk? Why did the founders choose the main activity that people with MS can't do? We hobble, limp, use walkers and use wheelchairs. Isn't it a bit of a slap in the face to invite people to do the one thing we can't do? What if breast cancer awareness groups held wet T-shirt contests? How about dementia awareness groups hosting trivia games? I mean, come on people!

How about an MS Parade? People living with MS could ride in cars and wave. How about an MS music festival: invite people to listen to various bands, while collecting donations and educating the public on the disease? It seems as though more thought could have gone into it.

Nevertheless, I tried to shake the fact that I'd only learned to walk again a few months prior. A severe lesion had caused me to lose all feeling on my left side and my brain couldn't tell my left leg to walk the way it used to. It had taken months to rebuild the muscle I'd lost and to be able to walk without a walker. My goal was to walk halfway.

It was empowering to follow the long line of MS supporters in various-colored shirts, carrying posters and balloons. Many healthy people jogged, but the majority meandered. My team spread out, moving at various paces.

My daughter walked next to me the entire time. She was not embarrassed by my limp or slow speed. She had witnessed how far I'd come. She wasn't concerned with how far and fast she could move. She seemed content at my side. Our silence symbolized the sadness of the disease, as well as the courage it took to live with it. Our smiles were from accomplishing this feat together. This beautiful, young lady remained close to me physically, mentally and emotionally.

I hate that Missy barged into my life. But if she hadn't, my daughter wouldn't have blessed me with the memory of "Janelle's Journey."

Change of Plans

As a child, if someone asked, "Janelle, what do you want to be when you grow up?" I'd respond with, "Anything but a teacher." I was not one of those little girls who played "school" growing up and always knew she'd want to be a teacher. But in a roundabout way, I entered the teaching profession. I ultimately discovered my life's passion.

I enjoyed every minute teaching reading to fifth graders. There were so many interesting discussions to be had when reading a story aloud together. One time, after Missy started coming to fifth grade with me every day, a student came to an unfamiliar word.

"Mrs. Sims? What does ree-sil-ent mean?" asked a student.

I responded, "Oh, *resilient.* It means to come back after a setback. For instance, in the spring, fresh baby flowers are beginning to bloom. Suddenly, they are pounded by snow or hail. They're left wilted and crumpled. But after some time and with sunlight, they begin to perk up and bloom again. They are *resilient.*"

A girl in the back suddenly shouted, "Mrs. Sims! That's *you!* You've been sick and have had trouble walking. But you don't give up. You keep working every day to get better and here you are!"

A chorus of "Yeah!" went around and suddenly, my room full of 10-year-olds began clapping.

I was speechless. Tears filled my eyes. I'd been working all year to teach them as much as I could and little did I know, I was teaching them more than reading strategies and comprehension techniques. Missy and I were teaching them about life.

I had planned on eventually becoming one of those seasoned and admired gray-haired teachers.

One day, during my teacher prep time, while my students were in music class, I checked my voicemail.

"Hi, Janelle. This is the nurse from the doctor's office. We have the results of your MRI. You have two more active lesions. The doctor wants to start you on a round of IV steroids as soon as possible." This meant no working and at-home nursing care for three days.

During that time, I met with my neurologist. "Janelle, I know how much you love teaching, but I'm concerned about your health. We have to try to get your MS under control. Teaching seems to be too hard on your body. Not to mention all the exposure to germs, which triggers your immune system," she said.

She looked at my husband. I felt double-teamed.

"I agree, Baby. You work too hard and your health is declining. I really want you to stop working and take care of yourself. I'm worried that something even worse may happen to you, if you don't."

This couldn't be happening. I'd never once considered leaving the career I loved. I wasn't ready.

I agreed to take a temporary leave. My doctor and husband seemed relieved and the paperwork began.

An Entertaining Way to Cope

I had no idea that I would never set foot in a classroom again.

For this, more than for anything else, I hated Missy. Being a teacher was my identity. It was in my blood and Missy took it away. She wanted me all to herself. She made sure that my focus remained on her every single day.

In return for my agreeing to rest, she began to lay off hurting my brain the way she had been doing. Instead, she broke my heart. But, not wanting Missy to win, I found the positive in the situation. Instead of remaining sad about my loss, I chose to be grateful for what I'd had. I had been blessed with nine years as a teacher to so many incredible students. They made me laugh. They made me proud. They taught me so much about myself. I want to believe that I made a positive impact on each of them. I worked alongside the most supportive, hardworking teachers in the world, who came to be precious friends. I loved the school I worked in and wouldn't trade that school, that staff, those students, or those memories for anything. Although Missy ended my career, she cannot take the precious memories I made. I choose to be grateful for that.

A Penny from Heaven

My husband hated dogs. He would even refuse to watch dog movies and dog commercials. If a dog approached him on a sidewalk, he'd get nervous and move away from it. He was somehow convinced that all dogs do is bark, poop and bite people. Getting a family dog was out of the question. My kids had begged for one for years. He would threaten that if we got a dog, it would disappear in the middle of the night and "be taken to a farm."

By this point, I was adjusting to my MS diagnosis. I was beginning to accept that my life would contain only the most important of activities, and that I would be good friends with my bed. I had learned how to record mindless television shows as entertainment for the hours I would spend resting.

Meanwhile, my family remained busy. My daughter was working and going to school. My son was constantly practicing sports and keeping up with middle school. My husband worked long hours and balanced it with his own downtime.

That left me sitting at home on my bed with Missy.

The idea popped into my head. *"A dog. Get a dog."*

I mustered up my courage and approached my husband.

"I want a dog. I'm home alone all the time while everyone else gets to have an active life. I need something more in my life. I want a dog," I pleaded.

An Entertaining Way to Cope

His response, "Do whatever you want but I don't want any part of it. I'm not taking care of it, or paying for it, and I don't want it anywhere around me. And you know I'm allergic to them."

"I'll get a hypoallergenic dog that doesn't shed," I added.

He said "fine" the way spouses say it, meaning, "Don't you dare or you will regret it." Visions of him retaliating by buying a new motorcycle, or even worse, "taking the dog to the farm" flashed through my mind.

I decided to explore my options. I consulted friends as to where and how to find a dog.

Within an hour, a friend began texting me about a Shih Tzu she'd adopted a few months prior. The dog didn't seem happy with her family. They had two other dogs and four children. She thought the dog would be happier in a household like mine. Everything she said about it checked off all my boxes: She was medium-sized, calm, three years old, crate-trained, and potty-trained. My friend was heartbroken to give up her dog, but she wanted to do what was best for the dog.

I asked the dog's name. *Penny.*

My jaw dropped.

Pennies were special in our family. My husband's father carried coins at all times. He enjoyed tossing coins for the children to run and find. Even after he made his trip to heaven, he has found a way to leave coins for us to find. We frequently find change in odd places that we believe is his way of saying hello.

I immediately phoned my husband and blurted the details about the dog. I waited silently and hesitantly for his response.

"It sounds like the perfect dog."

"Well, there's more. And I think it means something. Her name is Penny."

More silence.

He finally said, "She sounds like a gift from my dad."

I said, "I think so, too. Can we meet her?"

Two days later the cute, little, grey and white Shih Tzu confidently pranced through our front door. She immediately settled in my husband's designated spot on the couch where *none* of us were allowed to sit. And she never left.

Most surprisingly, she quickly wrapped my husband around her paw. He was instantly in love with her. He can't wait to come home and see...the dog. If I can't find him, I'll eventually find him on the floor cuddling...the dog. When I hear him talking sweetly to someone, I'll discover he's with...the dog.

Well that was easier than I thought it would be. Thanks to my father-in-law and his pennies.

Grey and white, she doesn't resemble a penny at all. We decided that since she'd only had that name a short while and we had received the message from Greg's dad, we could rename her.

An Entertaining Way to Cope

Greta.

She looked and acted like a Greta. She believed she was a queen, deserving of all attention at all times. Deserving of the softest bed, the best food and the most high-quality treats. She had a variety of collars to match seasons and holidays. Yes, spoiled.

But she filled a void in my life. I'd lost my health, my energy, some friends and even my career. Now I had this four-legged, tail-wagging, ear-bouncing dog who loved the fact that I rest a lot. I'm never alone (even in the bathroom) and she brings joy to my life.

So, although I don't want Missy in my life, she is responsible for Greta having made her way to me. For that, I'm grateful.

Working Like a Dog

I know people with MS sometimes benefit from service dogs. I wasn't to a point in my illness to want to pursue this but our family had been recently blessed with our dog, Greta, and I was beginning to notice some things.

I already knew I was "her person." She'd get excited to see my husband and kids and would demand they pet her. But, she *had* to know where I was at all times. I was her favorite. When it was possible for her to be next to me, she was.

We were fortunate that she rarely barked. She'd gently growl if she wanted to be petted and wanted table scraps. But she could also "talk," as I called it. She'd get my attention, look me straight in the eye and say, "Roo-or-roo-roo." She was definitely trying to tell me something.

Similar to a mother trying to figure out what her toddler wants, I'd run through the basic options: "Do you need to go outside? Are you thirsty? Do you want to play?"

If I had asked the right question, she would have let me know by jumping and getting excited. Instead, each question was answered with a stare and more "talking." Meanwhile, I'd grow frustrated as I'd be in the middle of doing laundry, cleaning the kitchen, or picking up the house. I didn't have time to play *Twenty Questions* with a canine that had a limited vocabulary. I tried to ignore her and continue with my chores. She followed me and continued to "talk" to me.

"What do you want?!" I shouted.

She stared up at me.

"Do you want to get on Mommy's bed?"

I'd finally asked the right question. She nodded her head, sneezed and happily trotted to my bedroom. I helped her onto the bed and left to go back to my duties.

She jumped down and followed me, continuing her dialogue.

"Roo-rrr-roh."

"What now?!" I shouted in frustration.

I stomped back to the bedroom with her and put her on my bed. She stood and stared at me. I went over to my side of the bed and laid down. Suddenly, she walked over, found a spot and with a heavy sigh, laid down in a ball. Content.

This is what you wanted? For me to lie down with you? Hmm. Now that I think of it, I'm really tired. My body is aching. I'm more fatigued than I realized. Maybe I should rest.

This scenario played out over and again. It wouldn't happen every day, just some days. However, I started to notice that she'd exhibit this behavior only when I'd been doing too much, and my body had grown tired. It's as if she could pick up on my fatigue before I could.

She'd happily nap without me on a regular basis. But when she'd follow me, talk to me, and demand that I lie down with her, she was always right. Even my family saw it.

"Mom, she's doing that thing where she follows you and talks to you. You must be tired. Go lie down."

Greta also had a knack for monitoring my body heat. People with MS have to be careful about becoming overheated. I tended not to notice until severe symptoms crept in. I start to lose my vision, my left leg becomes stiff and I might drool and slur my words. This heat-loving Texas girl has never met a sunny, hot, and humid day she didn't love. Until Missy moved into town.

I still love the heat, but Missy doesn't. She must originate from the North Pole. Nah. On second thought, there's no way Missy and Santa Claus share anything in common.

Greta, my nap-loving, don't-wake-me-unless-food-is-involved dog turns into a frolicking energized puppy when we get our Colorado snows. She romps and digs in the snow all day, no matter how much ice clings to her fur. But heat? Nope. She hates it. And she seems to know when it's too hot for me as well.

She might be enjoying a nap somewhere but she'll get up and find me. I'm usually doing dishes or sweeping the floor or some other I-was-born-a-girl-so-it's-my-job duty. She'll come over to me, look and pant. It's not even a real heavy breathing, tongue-drooping pant. It's a fake pant. Her mouth opens and she simply shows her tongue with a "huh-huh," then looks at me.

"Are you hot, Greta?" I stupidly ask. How can she be hot? She's inside the house and has been napping.

Then I realize *I'm* hot. I've been working in a stuffy house with little airflow. I'm even slightly sweating. Oops.

I've overheated without noticing and sure enough, my symptoms begin to show.

"Okay, Greta. I'll get some ice water and a cooling pack and sit with you." She happily sneezes and heads back to the bedroom.

How does she know this stuff? She's not a trained service dog by any means. However, she naturally alerts me to fatigue and body temperature issues. This makes her *my* service dog.

See Missy? You are a villain who seeks to destroy me, but my tiara-wearing Shih Tzu is my sidekick, with powers to protect me from your sneak attacks.

Remember

"Oh my gosh! Tomorrow is Father's Day! We don't have any gifts! What are we going to do? What stores are still open? What should we get? How did this happen?"

It was a Saturday night in June. We'd been watching TV and it was close to time for bed.

My son smirked at me. "Uh, Mah-um?" questioned my son.

Oh, no. What had I said or done now? I knew when "mom" was stretched into several syllables, it meant Missy had made me do something stupid. She had that way with me.

"What?"

"Mom, we bought his gifts yesterday," he calmly reported and stifled a chuckle.

"We did? What did we get?"

"We got accessories for his new bike. Remember?"

I hated that word. Missy had singlehandedly taken "*remember*" from my vocabulary. The girl who could beat anyone at the game *Memory*. The student who could memorize anything her teacher assigned. The one who never forgot dates or, much to my husband's frustration when it came to marital squabbles, things people said and did. But Missy found making me forget little things I'd recently said and done hilarious. My childhood? No problem. Last year? Easy. Yesterday? Nope, gone.

"Where are they?!" My frantic reaction could have stemmed from my feeling confused and inadequate.

He said, "We hid them."

Oh, crap. That's not good! I have no idea where I put them.

"Do you know where?" I asked.

"In the basement, under the stairs." Then the mental image of the wrapped packages slipped back into the holes of my memory. *That's right. I remember now.*

"From now on, don't ever let me hide anything. I'll never remember where I put it."

He snickered and I could see his ornery wheels turning. "Hmm, I could have fun with this."

"Don't you dare pick on a lady with a brain disease!" I laughed. "By the way, what's your name again?"

He knew this family joke. Ever since I'd forgotten my husband's name that time, we'd joked about my forgetting the kids' names as well.

Missy has caused a lot of laughter in our house. Don't get me wrong. She's caused plenty of tears as well. But once I learned to laugh at the things she causes me to say and do, it helps me hold a bit more power. I won't allow her to steal my joy.

A New Hobby

I needed another pastime. I had watched enough crime shows to know plenty about committing the perfect murder. (I've told my husband not to worry unless he sees me taking notes.) I loved to read, but I needed something else. Something new. Missy had taken my career, my love of dancing, my enjoyment of shopping and certainly my busy schedule. What was something new I could do while spending so much time in bed?

One day a friend called to invite me to her house for a knitting club.

Knitting? I'm only 40. Isn't there an age requirement for that? Don't I need bifocals and grandchildren? Is this the level Missy has sunk me to? Am I desperate enough to (gasp) knit?

It was hard to pass up the invitation when I heard that many of my closest friends with whom I'd taught were attending. I missed them terribly. I agreed to go.

Of course, Missy wanted to intrude on any scheduled activity. She tried to convince me that I was too tired and achy to have any fun. This was one of those times that I played her game for a while, setting aside all of my duties and remaining on my bed. I relaxed my whole body and did nothing for hours. Once she seemed to quiet down, I jumped (not literally, of course) out of bed, got dressed and prepared to leave.

Missy realized that I was sneaking away to have a bit of fun in my life, so she weighed down my arms and legs. For added persuasion, she took some of my peripheral vision. I felt myself bristle as I told Missy to *"Shut up and leave me alone!"*

(It's actually therapeutic for me to shout at her. It's empowering to hear my own voice standing up to her. If I ever actually hear her respond, well, I'll be looking for an additional diagnosis.)

It's just that I can't always let her win. I can't let her be my boss 24/7, even though she tries. Spending some time with my friends, albeit *knitting*, was something I wanted to do. I needed to do it.

I know I can't get away with this stubbornness often or for long. Missy will find a way to punch me squarely in the face and make sure she gets extended alone time with me. But I've learned that if I let her have her way for a while, go have some fun, and remember her again later, I can be okay.

Knitting is a lot harder than it looks. I found a new respect for those grandmas. Or maybe Missy makes it difficult. Trying to hold a needle and yarn in a hand I can't feel is an added struggle. As my friends were looping and tucking away, I was dropping loops and tying knots and even figured out a way to knit backwards.

I kept at it. Step by step, over and over, and I got the hang of it. I chose to celebrate with a sip of wine. I discovered that hip ladies knit while drinking wine and snacking. This was as wild as my life was going to get. I enjoyed funny stories and family updates.

Missy gave me tongue tingles, which was her way of letting me know I was too tired. I gathered up my yarn and needles and went home.

I practiced knitting a little bit every day. My piece was full of unintentional holes and for some reason it became wider and wider. However, I was glad to have something else to do with my time. Not only did I have evidence of productivity, but I felt a bit defiant because, although Missy had taken away my sense of touch, I was still knitting.

After I'd gotten the hang of it, I decided to choose a fuzzy purple yarn and make a scarf for my daughter. I was actually able to finish it rather quickly. I'm sure she'll never wear it but I encouraged her to treasure it. I explained that my fingerprints were on every stitch and each one contained my thoughts of her. Someday, when she doesn't have me, she can wrap that scarf around her and feel my hug.

I've been working on a blanket for my son for quite some time now. Knitting a blanket is like knitting four scarves at once!

I continued meeting with my knitting group, which was becoming more talking and eating than knitting. These times with friends and laughter refreshed me while simultaneously wearing me down, but it was worth it.

I have learned to pick my battles with Missy. I've learned that she doesn't play fair. She was never nice or forgiving. Ignoring her usually backfires in a major way. But when I need to stand up against her, I do. It is the only way this suffering can be bearable.

Spiritual Journey

I had only hours before been diagnosed with Multiple Sclerosis. I was in the hospital, hooked up to IV's, and still trying to make sense of what was happening.

I texted a few friends to tell them about my diagnosis. One of my closest friends responded with typical concern and compassion. She offered prayers. A few minutes later, she texted me again.

"You are being attacked by Satan. You need to pray and ask for forgiveness. You must not have your heart right with Jesus. Make sure to ask for Jesus to be in your heart. This is why this is happening."

I was stunned. I hadn't been diagnosed long enough to even consider the "why." Why me? What did I do to deserve this? In fact, I would ask these questions off and on for months. But at this point, it hadn't occurred to me that I'd caused this disease. I still didn't know much about MS. In the back of my mind, I knew that my spiritual life didn't have anything to do with it. But I had made some mistakes in my life that I regretted. *Was I being punished with this disease?*

I had grown up in a Christian household. I was active in the church youth group and choir. I spent every summer at a Christian camp. As a teenager, I directed the music at a small church. I knew the basics of the Bible and I was baptized and saved.

When I was diagnosed, I was less involved in church, but my heart and mind were still Christian. I was still a believer and I prayed; I just wasn't attending a church.

Could my dear friend be right? Just in case, I muttered a prayer from my hospital bed, demanding that Satan leave me alone and begging for Jesus to be in my heart and to heal me of this disease.

Guess what? Not only was I not healed, I never heard from my friend again. She'd been my closest friend for five years. Never once did she call, text, or visit. Her personal spiritual belief seemed to be that if I was sick, I had Satan in my life and she needed to stay away.

This loss was the first of many due to Missy entering my life. I struggled for a long time with not only the loss of a friendship, but with what she'd texted to me. Was I being punished for getting divorced? Was this because I didn't attend church enough? Why had God chosen this for my life?

I wished my sweet, Christian mother were still alive to help me with this. Even though she had suffered illnesses, she had always remained loving and faithful to God. She had been the epitome of a good Christian woman.

How did she do it? How did she handle feeling miserable every day yet still love God? Did she wonder why this happened to her? What got her through it?

I looked through her Bible to see if she'd marked any answers. I even contacted her closest friends to see if she'd shared any of her secrets with them. I was struggling.

One particular day, I yearned to watch old home videos. I'm nostalgic like that. Watching family movies and looking through photo albums has always been comforting to me. I went to the closet to look for the tub that contained the movies. I reached in.

Wait. What are those notecards mixed in with the videotapes? Where did they come from? I've never seen them before.

As I pulled the notecards out, I recognized my mother's handwriting. I trembled. I noticed that on each notecard, she had written a Bible verse. Each verse pertained to strength, courage, persistence, faith and hope. Each verse answered every question I'd wanted to ask her. The how, when and why of dealing with illness. They were exactly what I'd been searching for. To my recollection, I'd never seen these cards before. Of course, I liked to believe my mom found a way to give me what I needed in one last mother moment. It's okay if people are skeptical; disbelieving it's possible for this to have happened. The main point is that I received the answers I'd so badly needed. Those notecards remain on my bedside table.

It took months, maybe years, to heal my spiritual relationship. I eventually came to realize that God didn't do this to me, and I hadn't done anything to deserve it. I did continue to struggle with a guilt about not attending church. I wasn't ready to hear people glorifying and singing praises to a God who had allowed this to happen to me. He wasn't, in my mind, as awesome as I had previously thought.

I continued to try to renew my relationship with God. I prayed daily about anything and everything *except* MS. It was an off-limits topic. It was the area in which I didn't trust Him. My husband, children, finances, and safety, yes. MS, no. Maybe with more time.

For a long time I missed my friend. I couldn't believe I could lose such a dear friend simply because I was sick. I was shocked by her conviction in such beliefs.

Of course, I blamed Missy. I'd lost my good friend because of her. She'd come into my life and my friend had left. Missy was able to make me question everything I'd so firmly known to be true. How ironic that my mom in heaven was more powerful and more capable of reminding me what's real and true, than Missy.

River Walking

My healthy friends stay fit by hiking 14ers (it's a Colorado thing), kayaking, and walking. They do Zumba, aerobics and tae kwon do. Some of them are crazy enough to voluntarily attend torturous cross-fit classes. I listen to their funny stories as well as their fitness-finding, weight-losing, goal-succeeding stories. They have those cute workout clothes and shoes while I wear a shirt that says "My Yoga Pants Have Never Been to Yoga."

Although I can't participate in those activities with them, I knew some form of exercise and toning would be good for me. I settled on yoga. My mind believed that I could do every pose and every repetition announced by the instructor. My body (and Missy) disagreed. Unfortunately, my mind over matter won that day. I pushed myself to do everything the entire hour. I forced my body into contortions and held positions I'd never attempted before. Muscles were stretched and twisted and the pain convinced my mind that I was working toward a stronger and fitter body.

But that pain was actually Missy warning, "Whoooaaa, girl. You are going to pay for that! I don't know what you were thinking but you and I are going to have a lot of alone time over the next couple of days; you'll learn your lesson."

Yeah, Missy was unhappy with my yoga pants having the audacity to actually try yoga.

I was bedridden for a week. Yes, I had sore muscles, the same as anyone would expect for overdoing it on an exercise regime. But Missy threw in a body-flattening fatigue with it. It's as though I had used a week's worth of energy for one hour of yoga. I couldn't even hold up my arms to eat. I hardly had enough energy to chew the food that made its way to my mouth. Walking to the bathroom felt like I had two toddlers strapped to each ankle. When I'm that fatigued, I have trouble forming words and keeping saliva *inside* my mouth. Yep, the *corpse pose* was the only yoga I'd be doing for a while.

Several months later, the urge to exercise arose again. I knew to be more careful this time. I researched some classes at my local YMCA and decided to start with River Walking. This was a low-impact exercise that involved walking and stretching along with, and against, the current of a lazy river at the indoor aquatic center. Walking in water sounded easy enough. I seem lighter in the water so there was less weight to move around. The water would help to hold me up since my balance was wonky. I wouldn't overheat in the cool water. It sounded like a fit.

I shouldn't have been surprised to discover that this low-impact, slow-moving class was a favorite among older generations. When I showed up for my first class, at least a dozen senior ladies, and even a couple senior men, began entering the pool. I stuck out like a sore thumb with my bouncy brown (not gray) ponytail and two-piece (albeit modest) swimsuit. I should have invested in a two-sizes-too-big floral-printed one-piece in order to fit in better. I received a few half-smiles and curious "Who's the new girl?" looks. I kept to myself and began the warm-up, walking with the current in the lazy river. I quickly noticed that everyone seemed to know each other, and that this exercise class also served as their social time.

An Entertaining Way to Cope

From the side of the pool, the young instructor began shouting directions: "High knees and...go! Deep lunges and...go! Get ready to run in 3, 2, 1! Turn around (against the current) and march! Move those arms!"

I struggled to keep up. I stayed on the right side, like one should do when going more slowly in traffic, so that people can pass on the left. The entire group of elderly folk was passing me. Finally, a lady turned and shouted, "Honey, you should stay on the outside edge so people can go around you!" That would have been the "left lane." I quickly learned that river walking had different traffic rules.

I worked hard to stay ahead of the seemingly 95-year-old woman to maintain some dignity. I could feel myself begin to shake with fatigue. *How much longer do we have? What?! Is that clock right? Have we only been in class for 25 minutes?! I'm dying! There's no way I can last a full hour!*

"Excuse me honey," the 95-year-old said as she passed me on the right.

Finally, the instructor handed us pool noodles to sit on. *Oh, good. I can rest a little.* Nope. We had to straddle those pool noodles as if they were bicycle seats, and pedal our arms and legs in order to "bike" against the current. *Low impact, slow moving class, my ass!*

I was now out of breath, out of energy, out of strength but still not out of time. In this humiliating moment, Judy and Nancy got up the nerve to strike up a conversation with me. "Are you working off an injury?" one inquired. I guess that would provide a reasonable explanation as to why someone my age would willingly participate in this particular class. With nothing to be ashamed of, I smiled and said, "No. Actually, I have Multiple Sclerosis and I struggle to walk and keep my balance." The ladies' faces changed into sympathetic, understanding smiles. "Well, good for you for being here!" one said as the other reached for a high-five. Then they regained their pace and moved past me.

After one of the longest hours of my life, the instructor led us in some cool-down stretches. I made my way over to the stairs to climb out of the pool. On shaky legs, out of the buoyancy of the water, I was reminded of every heavy pound of my body. I wobbled into the locker room to shower and change with the old ladies who still had plenty of energy to laugh and carry on.

I dragged home, Missy in tow. She loved that I was exhausted. She chuckled at the way those senior citizens had lapped me around the pool. However, to my surprise, after some rest, I wasn't as sore as I'd expected. I was proud of myself for not having given up, and was hopeful that the class might help with my balance and strength. I decided to go back again a couple of days later.

On my second visit, I was greeted by some of the class members. Several ladies introduced themselves to me. Apparently the locker room gossip had informed them that I had MS, and this allowed them to accept my presence. A few of the ladies had relatives or friends with MS, and seemed to have had a glimpse of how difficult it is. They were supportive and encouraging.

I made my way into the pool and began warming up with walking laps. Knowing that my classmates knew about my MS enabled me to feel comfortable pacing myself and taking breaks as needed. No reason to compete! I entertained myself by eavesdropping on conversations around me. "Have you heard from Margaret?" "You wouldn't believe the vegetables in my garden." "Well at my next appointment, they are going to do some lab work." "This pain in my shoulder just won't go away."

At least this time, as they each passed me, they were nice enough to say hello and some even asked my name. The 95-year-old still called me "sweetie" as she passed me. Missy tried piggy-backing me and going under water to weigh my legs down, but I kept going. I lasted 35 minutes instead of 25 before checking the clock. During the noodle-riding, I allowed the current to let me "coast" now and then, which was actually fun. Again, Missy reminded me how tired I was after the class ended, but she backed off after some rest.

By my third class, I was no longer "the new girl." This seemed to signal to the men in the class that they were allowed to talk to me. There I was, walking laps, marching, lunging and side-stepping through the water with four pot-bellied men all around me. They talked about nothing but food. They clearly determined that it was their job to educate me on their favorite foods at their favorite local restaurants. "You must try the big burritos at the Mexican place down on Third Street. They are the best in town." The other men always refuted these comments. "Don't tell her that. If she's serious about Mexican food, she needs to go to Romero's." "You don't know what you're talking about. She needs to go to Roja's." Once in a while, a group of ladies would tread by us and say to me, "Honey, don't listen to a word they say. They're just causing trouble." I'd chuckle; the men would ignore them and move on to the topic of sub sandwiches.

This entertainment had a way of pushing Missy into the wake behind me. I didn't push myself as hard because, let's face it, those men were only in the class because their wives made them go. They couldn't care less if they completed anything beyond their daily word limit. However, I was still managing my version of a workout and felt good about it. It was nice to be included in the river-walking gang, even if they were all 30+ years older than I was.

Me and my group of seniors. An experience I wouldn't have enjoyed had Missy not come around.

Missy and Me

Let's do a tally: I've lost my career; I've lost some friends. I can no longer dance and can only barely play the piano. I can't eat my favorite foods because lying in bed doesn't burn enough calories. It takes too much energy to shop, hike, or picnic. I can't even enjoy a hot bath. I was intelligent, but now I can't remember what I did yesterday.

All of these things made me *me*. Who am I now? What is left of my identity?

"Oh, Janelle? Yeah, she's the one with MS." That would be how people knew me or identified me. Come to think of it, I never liked that I was described as the lady with curly hair and glasses. That conjures a less-than-pleasant image. You don't see super models on magazine covers with curly hair and glasses. You might see them on beauty magazines as a *before* picture, and then a stunning *after* picture shows her with a blow-out and contacts. But now that I'm becoming "the one with MS," I'd be grateful to go back to being "curly hair and glasses."

I'm proud to be a wife and mother. I take those roles seriously and passionately. But I also used to be a teacher, a life coach, a dancer, a pianist, and a fun person to be around. I've lost so much of who I was.

It would be easy to let Missy take me completely and become *all* of who and what I am. She makes her presence known wherever I am. I sway when I walk. My left foot drops with each step. My walker and foot brace function as a forehead stamp that reads: I have MS.

I can't do anything without Missy interfering.

I don't have MS in my dreams. And I have vivid, life-like dreams. In them, I'm always busy and active with nothing slowing me down. When I wake up, it takes all of half a second to remember that I can't feel my left foot under the covers. When I shift, I'm reminded that I can't feel the texture of the sheets. My aching muscles let me know I'm already fatigued and the day hasn't even begun. My dreams end and I wake to a nightmare. Missy sits on my body and shouts sarcastically, "Good morning!"

Getting out of bed and walking to the bathroom require constant concentration in order to convince my body to cooperate. Days that involve getting dressed and (gulp) taking a shower, require strict routines, accommodations and rest between activities. Missy pulls down my arms as I wash my hair. She makes sure I set the water to lukewarm, and she gets a kick out of tricking me into squirting body wash on my hair and shampoo on my pouf. (I will never forgive her for confusing the IcyHot and my toothpaste. Nobody deserves to have IcyHot in her mouth.)

She nags me all day, every day.

"You want to go out with friends? Then you will have to rest all day first. Your husband asked you on a date? Which dress shoes can you wear with your brace? Your son has a basketball game? I'll sit next to you in the warm gym and take away your vision."

Every decision about the future, such as where to retire, what type of home to live in, financial planning and future vacations require us to include Missy.

I'd read enough accounts of other personal battles with

MS to know what my future could look like. I was aware of how consuming Missy could be. I wanted to figure out how I could become *more* than Missy and me.

I had to be creative. What were some things I wanted to learn how to do? Was there anything about my personality that I wanted to change? What roles did I want to add to my newly-updated resume beyond wife, mother and Missy's best friend?

Time with my friends got the ball rolling.
"Janelle, you always have funny stories."
"I love the way you put things into perspective for me."
"You have such a way with words."
"You should write a book!"

I've always loved to read. I was considered a good writer in school. And writing *is* something that doesn't require much physical energy. I'll give it some thought.

Missy and me, an author. Hmm, I could live with that.

Bucket List

It's a common phrase: "I have MS, but it doesn't have me." How do I accomplish that?

First, make a list of the things I want to accomplish in life. What is on my bucket list? Write the list as quickly as possible and ignore the fact that Missy wants to be involved.

Then, consider the priority of each item.

Next, figure out how to make each one happen. Missy will try to convince me that I *can't* do many of these things. For now, ignore her and be clever about how to make things possible.

Then, alter my expectations. This doesn't have to mean lowering my expectations, just changing them. I might not do it the way I'd seen other people do it. I'd just have to visualize participating in each activity in whatever way I'd be physically capable of.

Lastly, make things happen sooner rather than later. No excuses. Time is not on my side.

Who would have believed I could add zip-liner to my identity *post diagnosis*? I always thought I'd get to zip-line someday, but I had put it off. This was important to me. I knew I'd regret not zip-lining during my lifetime. However, at this point, I wasn't healthy enough to do so... until I changed my expectations.

I researched zip-lining. I live in Colorado where there are plenty of zip lines. The problem is, they require hiking, climbing ladders and using lots of upper body strength to hold on and stop. I couldn't do those things. But then I found another place. They would take me to the top of a mountain in a truck, no hiking required. The harness fit around my legs and all I had to do was sit and fly out across the cable. No climbing, running, jumping or muscle use required. The next passage was close by without hiking or climbing. I was going to be able to zip line after all! It might not be as hard-core as some have experienced, or what I'd seen on television, but it was close enough to mark it off my bucket list. Missy wouldn't be able to take this particular dream from me.

My husband, kids and I were taken to the top of a breathtaking Colorado mountain. I looked at my husband and daughter bouncing along with me in the back of the truck. I looked at my son on what happened to be his birthday. I was overcome with the realization that I was going to experience this adventure with my family. Times like these had become few and far between.

Once we reached the top, I was helped out of the truck and to the platform. I was pleasantly surprised that I truly did not have to climb, hike or walk very far. My teenagers were hooked to cables dangling over a beautiful mountain valley. They sat in their harnesses and sailed quickly across, while shouting and waving.

It was my turn. Missy was in the back of my mind, worrying me that I would overdo it. But this was one of those times when I felt I'd done my best to get along with her. Again, I don't typically fight her or ignore her. I take her needs into consideration. I wouldn't allow myself to become overheated or fatigued, nor would I do anything rambunctious. I remained aware of all of this.

I stood on the edge of the platform, next to my husband. We could see the panoramic mountain view and the tops of the evergreen trees. The guides attached my harness, lowered me into a seated position and off I went! The breeze was in my face as I glided over the treetops. I couldn't help but shout "whoo-hoo!" and even heard my gleeful echo. In that moment, I was alone, no Missy with me. I felt normal. Healthy. I was enjoying life. Missy rarely allows those moments. I felt triumphant, as if this experience symbolically flipped Missy the bird.

Once I reached the other side, the guide caught me and stood me up. I got to zip across six more lines. On some, I'd pair up with my daughter or my son, and challenge them to a race. My husband and I would try a high-five as we sailed across together. They seemed to find joy in their own experiences, but also joy in watching me enjoy myself temporarily free from suffering or struggling.

It was a completely successful adventure; I have a memory that even Missy wouldn't be able to take away. I might have had to revise my bucket list once Missy moved in with me, but I wasn't going to give her the power of wadding it up and throwing it away.

Dancing

My husband was raised in a religion that disallowed dancing. He never attended a school dance, nor did he ever visit a nightclub. I, on the other hand, grew up two-stepping at family barn dances from the age of five. I loved the dance floor at every school dance, and wedding, and the town's street dance every fall.

Although my husband moved past his dancing-is-sinful belief, he hasn't learned to dance. If a good song comes on, he sits in his chair and bounces his arms to the beat, while cocking his head and sticking his tongue out of the corner of his mouth. That is the extent of his dancing talent. Early in our marriage, I would beg him to dance with me. He once agreed to take recreational ballroom dancing lessons. Since he has a music background and can find the beat, he discovered that he wasn't too bad at stomping out the moves as shouted by the dance instructor.

However, he never took me dancing.

During the first summer after my diagnosis, I could barely walk. My brain had to reteach the nerves in my left leg to walk again. I was very weak and very frustrated. I'm good-natured with the fact that my family uses humor to get through tough situations. My kids would challenge me to a race, or threaten to walk off and leave me somewhere. My husband chose this time in our marriage to say, "Baby, I feel like dancing," as he bounced up and down in place, "Let's go dancing," knowing full well that I couldn't. I responded with a smile, a bird, and a profane word. I knew he was kidding. He wanted to dance as badly as he wanted a bikini wax.

Fast forward a few years. My walking had improved. I still hobbled a little, had some foot drop and tired easily but that was my new normal. Medications seemed to be preventing any major flare-ups. I was getting used to the new normal, and thinking about my bucket list. One thing stood out to me. *Dancing.* I knew I had a strong possibility of soon becoming permanently disabled and wheelchair-bound. I didn't want to regret never having danced with my husband.

Our anniversary was approaching, so we had a dinner date beforehand to discuss how we wanted to celebrate. Neither of us wanted anything, and we agreed not to buy presents. I knew what I wanted to ask for, but I prepared for the rejection.

"I know what I want to do for our anniversary. For our whole marriage, I've given up a big part of what makes me, me. And that's...dancing. A few years ago, I never thought I'd be able to dance again. I could hardly walk. Now that I can walk, I want to go dancing with you before Missy makes that impossible. I want to create a memory of being in your arms and dancing with you. I want to go country dancing. I'd even settle for line dancing...no natural ability required."

I held my breath. He looked at me and paused. I threw in to seal the deal, "If I can learn to walk again, you can learn to dance with me. Just once."

He smiled. I had him. "Done," he replied, "I can do that."

After dinner we went to a thrift store and bought western shirts and cowboy boots. My husband was practically giddy. But not about dancing. He has an old suede cowboy hat with a real bullet hole shot through it, that he absolutely loves. And that I absolutely hate. It's a disgrace to my extended ranching family, and I had always refused to let him wear it in public. My anniversary present to him was allowing that gawd-awful hat on his head when we went dancing. (And I promised I'd cremate it with him someday when he passes.)

I knew Missy would be tagging along, all decked out in her plaid shirt, jeans and boots. But nobody would be asking her to dance. It would be one of those times that she'd sit off to the side of the dance floor, brooding in self-pity because I'd threatened her with my spurs.

Last Honeymoon

"Baby, I don't like the direction in which your health is going. I don't think we have much time left to travel and do things together like that. Would you go on one last romantic vacation with me?" my husband asked.

Of course I wouldn't turn down the chance to be alone somewhere with my husband, my best friend. But realizing that I was planning my *last* trip with him weighed heavily on my heart.

I knew I wanted a beach vacation. We'd been to Cancun, Mexico several years before. There were some good moments but apparently the "bottled water" was nothing more than Mexico water in bottles, and we spent much of our trip in the bed or bathroom. It hadn't quite checked off the romantic-beach-vacation bucket list box.

However, now that I had Missy traveling with me, medical care was an issue. I never know when Missy is going to cause another lesion in my brain to make me blind, lame or incontinent. I didn't want to struggle with language barriers with doctors or find myself in questionable medical facilities. Is Solu-Medrol a universal thing? I didn't want to chance it.

I considered a Hawaiian vacation, but the idea of traveling that far on a plane over an ocean freaked me out. I'd suffered from flare-ups that suddenly appeared and had needed immediate help. Being 30,000 feet over nothing but water was not a safe place for me. So, I needed a beautiful beach location stateside; we decided on Clearwater, Florida.

Knowing this might well be our last romantic vacation together, there was extreme pressure to make it perfect. What did I need to have on this trip in order to feel completely fulfilled? Sand, crashing waves, pina coladas, reading on the beach, romantic water-side dinners, all yes. Sightseeing? Shopping? Museums? Water Sports? You know what? No, that I didn't.

This was different from the "old Janelle." She would have wanted to do all of these things. She would've wanted to go and see and do everything. Was it because Missy was accompanying me on this vacation? She certainly had a way of making all of those things difficult, if not impossible. But when I honestly considered what would make me happy, Missy was not a consideration.

What I really wanted to do was to be with my husband in a relaxing, beautiful location. I wanted to lie in the sand next to him. I wanted to stroll along the beach hand-in-hand. I wanted to laugh and play in the waves with him. I wanted to talk with him over drinks and dinner. I wanted to soak in all of the time with him.

It wasn't that Missy took my desire for adventure. It was that Missy had taught me to prioritize. Being alone with my husband was what I wanted more than anything else. He was my priority. I didn't want to look back on this trip and remember an aquarium. I wanted to remember holding my husband's hand and staring into his eyes, as the sun set on the water behind him. Missy did that for me. Missy gave me that. It's one of the things for which I can be grateful to her.

Not This, But That

Although I've written poems over the years, I do not consider myself a poet. Poems sometimes form in my mind and drive me nuts until I write them down. I wrote a Mother's Day poem for my mom and a first birthday poem for my daughter. I wrote a poem or two for my husband for anniversary gifts. In the wee hours of the morning, after I'd received a call that my mother had passed away, a poem filled my mind that ended up as her eulogy. If I'd forced myself to sit and write a poem, I'd never have been successful. Poems had to come to *me*.

Missy is a night owl. She loves to keep my tired body awake all night. She excitedly makes my legs tremble, jerk, and ache. She intrudes in my thoughts to keep me from sleeping. She chatters and wiggles nonstop.

It was during one of these nights that I learned something about insomnia. I realized that it stood for: ***I'm Not Sleeping Or Merely Napping, I'm Awake!***

Missy takes credit for this acronym; she consumed my 2 a.m. thoughts upon this discovery.

I desperately wanted to sleep. I struggled to stay awake during the day, though Missy wanted me to nap, so that I could sleep at night. When I sleep, I dream and when I dream, I live a life without Missy. Oftentimes, I'm teaching again; I get to see my students and my teaching friends. I even look forward to all of the planning and grading. Then I wake to reality.

During one of my sleepless nights with Missy, a poem came to me. It's about how to get along with Missy.

Not This, But That

Not fearing the illness,
But figuring out how to live.
Not crying about the future,
But making the present as joyful as possible.

Not burning energy on anger or frustration,
But exerting energy on laughter and heart-to-hearts.
Not counting the hours spent with loved ones,
But making the hours memorable.

Not holding grudges designed to punish,
But forgiving quickly as to not waste precious time.
Not crying over the loss of relationships,
But cherishing those who love unconditionally.

Not worrying about what people think,
But considering the feelings of only those who matter.
Not hurrying for those who are waiting,
But taking a moment to laugh hysterically at something silly.

Not fretting about not being able,
But focusing on new interests and abilities.
Not maintaining composure,
But singing loudly to the radio.

Not feeling the embarrassment of being ill,
But feeling the pride of living each day.
Not grieving the shattered long term goals,
But realizing that current success prevails.

Not putting off dreams for a better time,
But making plans for dreams to come true.

Not hiding the struggle with a mask,
But inspiring with honesty about the fight.

Not taking pictures for storage,
But smiling often at precious memories.
Not striving to overachieve,
But settling with the success of the journey.

Not asking, "Why me?"
*But **discovering** "Why me?"*
Not regretting the "Nots,"
But choosing instead, the alternatives.

Nobody wants to live with sour old Missy. I hate her. However, since she has decided to be my Best Friend for Life, I must learn to make the best of it. This poem was meant to help the sweet people with MS see the possibilities of making lemonade out of lemons.

Perspective

After Missy and I had come to know each other fairly well, my neurologist insisted on a spinal tap just to check on some things. I'd heard horror stories of this procedure and I'd put it off as long as I could. After the appointment was set, I did what I always did: research the heck out of it in order to be as prepared as possible. I didn't need to know the doctor's role, but I wanted to know about people's personal experiences and consider advice they offered.

I was told to drink a lot of water and Gatorade in the days leading up to the spinal tap, to have migraine pain reliever on hand, and to be prepared to lay completely flat for 24-48 hours afterwards. I learned about spinal headaches and what to do if I developed one. I was as ready as I'd ever be for someone to stab a needle in my spine to draw out precious, necessary fluid.

I checked into the day surgery unit and put on the stiff gown. They came for me rather quickly, and into the operating room I went. I climbed onto the table, lay on my stomach, and they tilted the table to a 45-degree angle. The doctor and nurses were good about talking to me to keep me distracted from the procedure.

I could feel the pricks and burns from the numbing medication. As for the actual spinal tap, all I could feel was pressure on my lower back. It took about 20 minutes for the spinal fluid to fill the tube. Apparently spinal fluid doesn't quickly shoot into the tube, like blood does when it's drawn. I had to remain strapped at that 45-degree angle position, waiting for the tube to fill.

We talked about my kids most of that time. It's a subject that I can go on and on about. Talking about them makes me happy so it was a good way to pass the time. When the doctor was finished, the table was lowered, and I climbed back onto the gurney and was wheeled back into my curtained-off room. I had to lie flat for three hours before I could go home.

Once I got home, I stayed flat on my back except for quick bathroom breaks. I drank lots of liquids. Whenever I sat or stood up, a throbbing headache hit my head. This was expected so I'd lie back down as quickly as possible.

This headache, however, continued past the first 24 hours. And the next 24 hours. I could hardly move without an ice pick, jackhammer and iron vice simultaneously attacking my head. I took migraine medication, and after a few minutes of lying flat, the pain would subside. After a call to the hospital nurse, I was told that I was having a spinal headache and that I'd need to return to the hospital for a procedure called a blood patch. It seems that after a spinal tap, sometimes the hole in the spine doesn't close up and continues to leak spinal fluid, causing the headache. If blood is drawn and inserted back into the area of the tap, a scab forms on the hole and covers it up. It's supposed to bring immediate relief.

It was January in Colorado and we were being hit with a blizzard. The hospital was sixty miles away from home. I got in the car and tilted the seat back as far as it would go, but unfortunately, it wasn't far enough. My husband drove slowly on the snowy roads toward the interstate. Realizing I would have to suffer with this headache for at least two hours because it would take that long to get to the hospital on snowy roads, I decided I couldn't make it.

An Entertaining Way to Cope

I have a high pain tolerance. I've had numerous surgeries, physical therapy and health issues. I'd delivered a 10-pound baby through natural childbirth. Pain rarely debilitates me. However, a spinal headache is off the charts. It's not like any other pain that can be breathed through or distracted from. It was completely disabling. We decided to go to our local hospital's emergency room.

They were packed with people as usual. I went to the window, eyes closed, face scrunched, and explained that I was having a spinal headache due to a spinal tap a couple of days prior. I guess I was speaking a language they understood because they didn't question me further, nor did they ask me to "have a seat" in the waiting room. They had no beds available, but they had a reclining chair in the back of their office.

A nurse asked, "What is your pain level?"

"Ten!" my husband announced for me.

"It's a nine," I said. "Ten is reserved for amputation." I was in the most pain I'd ever experienced, but I still wasn't going to give it a ten. I figured something could always hurt worse than what I was feeling.

They promptly gave me IV fluids. They knew that being flat was what I needed and they repeatedly apologized for not having a bed available. My husband tried tilting my reclining chair back farther and it worked. He stood, bent over, pushing his arms into the head of my chair to hold it in that position. After a while, the headache began to ease.

We had to wait for surgeons to become available who could do a blood patch. After a while, my poor husband finally said, "Baby, I can't hold this chair down like this much longer. My arms are tired," regret filling his voice.

"Can you sit on it?" I asked.

"Let me see," he slowly turned around, placing his butt where his hands had been. The head of the chair was narrow. It was meant for a head. But we were going to make it hold a head and a butt. He sat down millimeters from my face. I could feel the edges of his jeans pockets on my cheek.

"Is this okay?" he asked.

I hesitated and chuckled. "Sure, but if you fart, I will never forgive you."

My humor seemed to ease some of his worry. "No promises," he joked.

We bonded in that position for quite a while. Nurses came to check on us and laughed. My entire chair was tilted back with my feet and its wheels in the air and my husband was basically sitting on my face. In sickness and in health, I suppose.

They finally had a bed open up and it went to me. Of course, I had to get up and walk to it, so the blinding pain shot back to my head. But at this point, I had perspective:

This was going to go away. We knew what the cause was and how to fix it. Tolerating this pain was a breeze compared to how I felt on a daily basis. My daily pain was not to this intensity but it was chronic, with no reason and no cure.

Knowing this pain had an end in sight was all I needed in order to be able to endure it.

Two of the nicest surgeons came for me. They didn't question me. They knew that having a spinal tap could cause this headache and that a blood patch was the answer. Unfortunately, the procedure required me to sit up and lean over a table. One doctor slowly drew blood from a vein in my hand then passed it to the doctor behind me, who inserted it near the spinal tap site.

It took longer than usual because my blood dripped slowly into the vial. The doctor in front of me apologized. The doctor behind me apologized for how long it was taking and thanked me for being cooperative.

I explained, "Guys, this is nothing. I can stay like this and put up with the pain for however long you need. I know there's an end to it. It *will* go away. I have Multiple Sclerosis so I struggle with pain and disability all day, every day and with no cure. That's what gets frustrating and exhausting. Believe me, I'm okay and you're okay."

They were both silent for a moment. Then one heart achingly muttered, "I'm so sorry to hear that," and the other one remained silent as they passed a sympathetic look between them. I could tell that my statement had impacted them. I doubt they dealt with MS very often. It seemed that this blood patch mission took on a whole new meaning for them; they wanted to become my heroes. They wanted to take this pain away, realizing it was a little thing they could do to ease my suffering. They worked diligently and carefully.

After a while, the pounding, stabbing and squeezing in my head began to disappear. It had worked. I had to lie down in recovery for a while. My lower back cramped from the procedure but this was normal and was nothing compared to the pain I'd been in before.

One of the surgeons returned to me. He pulled up a stool and sat next to my bed. He was somber.

"I have to tell you. My best friend and roommate was diagnosed with MS while we were in college. I watched him struggle and suffer. I watched him lose everything he loved in life. There was nothing I could do about it. There was not one thing I could do to ease his pain or to help him continue to live his life. I was there for him as much as I could be, but I couldn't really help him. I've always struggled knowing that. He passed away from MS complications when he was still very young. When you said you have MS, I suddenly felt his presence. I could feel him next to me. I felt like helping you was, in some way, helping him like I'd never been able to do. He was proud of me. He was happy that I was able to relieve your pain. I can't relieve your MS, but doing the little bit I could meant the world to both of us. I wanted to tell you that. I was definitely not expecting this kind of thing to happen when I came to work today. It seems we both received some healing today."

Missy strikes again. She causes agony, physically and emotionally, to not only her "friends," but to those around them. Yet in that moment, she had singlehandedly been the cause of years' worth of healing for this doctor. If

Missy and I hadn't been in that emergency room that day, he wouldn't have received the closure that he had so desperately needed. Yet again, Missy and I were a good team.

Spoons and Batteries

Having a limited amount of energy is common among those of us with MS. Some refer to energy quantity as "spoons" and only having a certain number of spoons each day to put toward activities. Some people compare it to a cell phone battery; activities require different amounts of battery life and batteries have to be recharged often. These are great mental images and helpful in relaying our experience to healthy people.

Although they are good guidelines, Missy doesn't seem to follow these expectations in our relationship. I can wake up in the morning without spoons or battery charge. Missy rolls over in bed and says, "Let's just spend the day in bed." She'll add anchors to my limbs and weights to my eyelids, leaving me with no choice but do what she says. I've tried narcolepsy medications, and although they keep me awake, they don't provide my muscles with any more energy.

Prioritizing can help at times. Missy is protective of her time with me. If I want to go out with my husband, to knit with my friends or to spend time with my children, I have to spend one-on-one time with Missy first, resting and relaxing. I have to look at the dirty laundry and the dishes that are piling up, and know that for today, being with my family or friends is the priority and household chores can wait. (I swear Missy must have a secret way she breeds laundry and dishes, because if I take a day off, they multiply exponentially.)

Simply getting out of bed, getting dressed and even putting on shoes require spoons or battery charge. A shower is an activity for me, just as date night or a doctor's appointment is, and must be prioritized and worked around with rest. I can do chores *or* go somewhere each day, but not both.

Missy jumps on my back and wraps around my legs. She sarcastically shouts, "Let's go!" and giggles with delight when each step feels like trudging uphill in peanut butter. After a few steps, she adds an aching pain to my muscles, as if I'd climbed several flights of stairs. As she keeps piggybacking, her weight causes my muscles to tense and shake with exhaustion. I can even get out of breath, as if I'd been doing Zumba instead of merely walking.

Can you remember holding up your arm in elementary class to get your teacher to call on you? You'd hold it straight up, waving your hand. She'd call on other people and you'd keep your arm up. Your arm started to hurt so you'd prop it up with the hand and elbow of your other arm. You'd keep it in the air. Your arm would get heavier and sink lower. It would be in front of you instead of up in the air. (By the way, as an elementary school teacher, I can tell you that we do not purposely cause arm fatigue as a cruel joke. In fact, I trained myself to call on the hands reaching straight in front, before the hands straight up, because I knew those kids had been waiting awhile.) Eventually, your arm drops and gives up before you do. If you're really eager, you'll switch to the other arm and repeat the process.

Missy has perfected this hand-in-the-air fatigue and can make it happen in seconds. If I want to fold a towel, I grab the corners, reach out, and hold it up. Missy hangs from my arms causing them to ache, quiver and promptly drop. My towel is folded only in half at this point. I rest my arms at my sides. When Missy stops paying attention,

I reach back up and quickly fold the towel in half again. Within a split second, Missy is onto me and yanks my arms back down. I rest them again. I just need to fold this towel one more time to consider it folded. Up again quickly and fold and drop. One towel down and Missy looks forward to playing our game over and over again.

As a creature of habit, who's been folding laundry for decades, I naturally fold laundry a certain way. I kept trying to fold laundry as I always had even once Missy had come to stay. I don't know why I struggled for so long before considering a different method. Stubbornness, maybe? Here's what I eventually discovered: Gravity is my friend. Folding laundry on a table requires significantly less energy than folding it in the air with my arms held out. I fold the towel corners together while the *table* is holding the towel. Not Missy and not me. I fold all my laundry fairly easily and quickly with this method. Missy pouts in the corner since she no longer gets to play her game.

I've discovered several tricks like this along my MS journey. Cooking, driving, typing, and so on. Anyone who lives with Missy will need to be creative in order to outsmart her. Just the other day, my husband and I were walking across a parking lot heading to a store. I noticed him nudging me to the side but the entrance was directly in front of me.

"Why are you pushing me to go that way?" I asked.

"Because the sidewalk is over there," he replied.

Such a natural, normal answer that seems to make sense.

But, to me?

"Do you know how many more steps it'll take to get to that sidewalk?" I asked. "Those are steps I'll need once I'm in the store. I can't waste them walking over to a sidewalk. Take the direct route."

"Hmm. I hadn't thought of that," he said. Healthy people rarely do.

If Missy has a certain number of spoons per day, she hasn't informed me of the number. If she has a certain battery charge percentage, it fluctuates daily. I've had to evaluate her moment by moment. My energy level seems to follow her mood. Is she hot and cranky? Overtired and frustrated? Is she stubborn and mean? Complacent then vindictive? What I'll be allowed to do each day is all a result of her mood. The more I relearn how to do things on a daily basis and evaluate Missy's mood, the better I get along with her.

Physical Therapy

"I'm going to prescribe physical therapy for you," said my neurologist. *Okay. Been there, done that.*

I'd seen several physical therapists for MS by this point. Usually they seem to specialize in injuries or post-surgeries.

MS is quite different.

My first physical therapist at least acted like he was familiar with MS. He could tell that my left leg was weak. Due to childhood scleroderma, my left side has always been smaller and weak. Missy had attacked that side of my body, so my left leg was even weaker and more atrophied than ever. The therapist watched me walk a few times. He noticed I had foot drop. He gave me a few exercises to try, like lunges and heel lifts, and sent me home.

The next week, I was scheduled to work with the physical therapy assistant. She was less than knowledgeable about MS.

"Okay! Let's start out on the exercise bike and see if you can go for 15 minutes!" she smiled and encouraged.

Lady, you obviously have no clue. I can get on that bike and I can darn well pedal for 15 minutes. One, because my right leg will take over when my left leg tires and two, because I have enough strength and energy to do that. What you don't get, is that after those 15 minutes, I will not be able to walk. I will not have energy to do anything else. For this body, riding that bike for 15 minutes equals a prescription for watching hours upon hours of predictable Hallmark movies.

Is this an effective use of my energy? Nope. But the forever do-what-I'm-told cooperative soul says, "Okay!" also with a smile.

I knew at that point, I would never go back. It was not my responsibility to educate the professionals charged with helping me. I left a message for my neurologist's medical assistant and explained that the therapists didn't seem knowledgeable about assisting someone with MS. She decided to send me to a different physical therapist.

The next physical therapist tried to understand MS by way of constantly comparing it to his wife's rheumatoid arthritis. I could tell he meant well and I was willing to give him a chance.

He assigned a list of exercises for me to do at home. He insisted on using my phone to record me doing various exercises so that I'd remember how to do them at home.

Dream shattered.

Most people have attempted to follow the instructions of various professionals through television and fitness routine videos. I was young, but I had sure enjoyed *Sweatin' to the Oldies* with Richard Simmons. When I grew older, I played and replayed the aerobic videos led by beautiful, perfect fitness trainers. Nothing bounced or jiggled on them that wasn't supposed to bounce or jiggle. I'd follow along in my living room believing that I looked just like them. In my mind, I had the grace, agility and body that they had. I have followed various yoga instructors' shows believing that my positions were as elegant and as poised as was theirs.

It took a physical therapist and my own phone to jolt me into the harsh reality of what my body actually looks like in these positions. I was nowhere near elegant, agile, or even fit. My awkward body leaning this way and that was far more pitiful than what my mind had imagined. It didn't help that we were in a small room and the close-up angles did nothing to flatter my figure. Lunging right and left in my t-shirt and baggy athletic shorts on that screen, I looked nothing like I did in my mind. And don't think any leotards or tights could have helped me at all. Nobody would want to watch those videos, least of all me.

Nevertheless, I went home and did as I was told, minus watching the videos. The next week, he timed me doing several exercises.

"I want you to stand up and sit down 5 times in a row and I'm going to time you," he said.

Always the obedient overachiever, I was game. Stand up and sit down five times. The first one went well. Then the left side of my body started to fatigue and I had to compensate with my right side. But that didn't stop me. I went as quickly as I could, so proud of myself.

"Okay. Stop. That was 21 seconds," he reported.

"What's the goal supposed to be?" I asked.

"Six seconds," he said.

What the heck? Ego officially crushed.

"Now I'll time you walking down this hallway and back," he directed.

Determined to reach whatever goal he had in mind, I focused all my attention as I walked down that hall. I had to concentrate on telling my left foot to pick up, my leg to move forward, and my knee to bend, as fast as I could. I got to the end and turned around.

He chose that moment to say, "You're doing good. Keep coming."

And...my concentration was interrupted. My leg bent, buckled and dropped all at once and I stumbled. It took time to correct my balance and get my rhythm back. I kept stepping the best I could, trying to reach the imaginary finish line.

"That was good," he said. "Let's try it again."

What's he trying to do to me? I haven't briskly walked down a long hallway in years (unless a restroom was involved). Now he wants me to do it twice? I could already feel my leg begin to tremble. But as usual, I sucked it up, determined to be successful at whatever was asked of me. I walked down and back.

"Okay! Your times were 28 seconds and 36 seconds. 12 is an average number."

I'm used to being above average but this isn't what I had in mind.

"You see, your body will get its muscle back, and the more you work, the faster you'll get back to normal."

And…you're fired. You must have been absent from physical therapy school when they covered debilitating diseases such as Multiple Sclerosis. I'm not going to waste my time trying to educate you on how MS works. The fact that you think it's possible for me to get back to "normal" shows how little you understand. You're even stupider (and I only use that made-up word to emphasize my point) to think that the more I work, the better. Dude, the more I work, the longer I'll need to recover in bed.

I plastered on my fake smile, thanked him for his time, and lied to him about scheduling another appointment. And for the record, due to his stretches, strengthening exercises and several timed sequences, I could hardly move for a week. My muscles were so fatigued, stiff and sore. He could take that stopwatch and shove it….well, you get the idea.

So when my neurologist suggested yet again that I should go to physical therapy, I was about as thrilled as a dog going to get neutered. But I never want to be accused of not giving my all to be as healthy as possible, so I agreed.

The appointment would be at yet another new place. The first visit was a consultation. To my shock, the physical therapist was very knowledgeable about MS, and had experience providing therapy to patients with MS. I was actually looking forward to receiving her help.

The following week, I went to my first appointment. She carefully watched me walk down the hallway to the exercise room. She noticed every little movement *both* of my legs were making. She had me stand on a pillow to identify issues with balance. I wobbled around and grabbed the bars to keep from falling.

An Entertaining Way to Cope

Who knew I couldn't stand on a pillow?

In fact, I wondered if it was normal to be able to stand on a pillow without wobbling. I made her do it and sure enough, she stood on it easily.

She had me lie down. Finally! Something I could do! She put a pool noodle on the table and I was to lie on the noodle with it running up the center of my back.

I fell to the left. I fell to the right. I worked and worked, trying to stay on top of that pool noodle.

Holy hell. I can't even be successful at lying down!

This exercise showed her that I had no core strength, as well as significant balance issues.

The next activity was to simply sit across from her and follow her finger with my eyes. I was successful for a little while and then the background became blurry and I was dizzy.

Oh my gosh! How do I get dizzy while sitting down?!

I'd had issues with dizziness. Walking through the grocery store, Missy would put me on the Tilt-a-Whirl and I'd have to stop in my tracks. I frequently shouted at her to "Stop the ride! I want to get off!"

My new physical therapist discovered that, due to a lesion in my occipital lobe, my eyes were weak and were not tracking the way they should. She gave me eye exercises. (My kind of exercises. No sweat or heavy breathing required.)

119

From then on, if Missy took me for a ride, all I had to do was focus my eyes on a single object and the ride would stop. Missy pouted and called me "no fun."

I continued with this physical therapist for several months. I learned so much about retraining muscles, improving balance and conserving energy. No longer did I feel inept. I felt I was finally taking the controls away from Missy and doing something to once again control my own body.

A Cane

"You need to get a cane," my physical therapist casually said, as though suggesting that I get a new pair of earrings.

Yeah, sure. I'll get right on that. Can't wait. How exciting.

Nope. Not gonna happen.

I'm already struggling with the fact that I'm officially "retired" from my teaching career, I knit for fun, and I can no longer walk without supportive sneakers. I'm 40! Somehow, for me, over-the-hill meant plummeting down the other side at breakneck speed and slamming into an old folks home. Before I knew it, dinner would be at 4 p.m., bedtime at 7:00 and I'd soak my teeth in a glass.

A cane?!

She tried reasoning with me as to how much it would help me get around. She was concerned with my good leg and what would happen to it if I kept putting all of my weight on it. She said Walmart had canes.

Every week she suggested it; every week I ignored her. One day I happened to walk past the canes in the store and I forced myself to look at them. I couldn't touch them, but I looked. I could think of many things I'd rather spend my money on.

She asked me about the cane again the next time. I shared how I couldn't force myself to pick it up and carry it to the check-out. I'd rather buy a rattlesnake.

"You can always order one online."

Hmm. Online shopping. Now she was piquing my interest.

There was no commitment in browsing online. I enjoyed researching the reviews and options. I was pleasantly surprised that canes came in different colors and patterns. Maybe a cool color would make me look cool walking with it.

Probably not.

I liked the ones that could stand on their own. The last thing I needed was to constantly have to bend over to retrieve it every time I let it go. I found a sparkly purple cane that seemed to fit me (if that's possible). I found it far easier to place it into my virtual cart than into a real one. Before I knew it, the cane was purchased.

I was able to forget about it. And then it arrived on my doorstep.

Well, I'm stuck with it now. I officially have a cane.

Missy and my therapist were happy with my purchase. Missy liked the satisfaction of making me need such a humiliating device, and my physical therapist was excited to teach me how to use it. Images of swinging my shiny purple cane around and smacking people upside the head with it, were the only things making *me* happy.

Missy wasn't pleased when she realized how much the cane helped me. She found it more difficult to make me trip and fall and I could move farther and more quickly with it. Over time, realizing how much Missy hated it, made me like it (sort of).

Shoes

I began to notice that hot dates with my husband
had turned into going to my doctors' appointments
together. We'd always prided ourselves on that fact that
we prioritized our marriage and scheduled weekly date
nights. We'd make the plan, schedule a babysitter, get
dressed up and enjoy an evening out together. It was
always so refreshing to talk uninterrupted and to be
reminded of how much we enjoy each other's company.
We could talk and talk. (Well, I'm the chatterbox and can
ramble on about every detail of every minute event in my
daily life, while he, the psychotherapist, listens intently as
he does for a living.) We'd make each other laugh about
ridiculous things. We'd hold hands when we walked and
enjoy being in love.

However, with him driving me all over the state to medical
specialists, our "hot dates" had become where-should-
we-eat-while-we're-here-for-a-doctor. We tried to make
the best of it. We always enjoyed being together, even if it
wasn't necessarily romantic.

During one out-of-town appointment, we had time to kill
before my visit. We decided to walk around a mall. The
fact that my husband suggested it should have made
me check him for fever or mental illness. He hates
shopping. He hates malls. He's had 60 years to perfect
the throwing of the toddler tantrum, when being forced
into shopping. But there he was, suggesting we walk
around the mall. I jumped at the chance. (Figuratively
speaking. These wobbly legs can't jump.) As it was early
on a weekday, the mall was fairly quiet. He was patiently
walking alongside me, while my left foot dragged and my
leg wobbled.

We came upon a shoe store and a pair of shoes caught the attention of both of us. They were tennis shoes with small stripes of hot pink, neon green, turquoise, black and yellow. We'd never seen such fun-looking shoes before. My husband excitedly suggested, "You need to go try those on."

I wasn't looking to buy anything, but what woman is going to turn down that offer? We went inside and found the shoes in my size. I put them on and was pleased with the fit and comfort. These were not the typical white leather shoes. They were soft and bright-colored.

My husband, who always has great taste, insisted that we buy them. And just like a little kid, I wore my new shoes out of the store.

We went to the doctor's appointment and at least three people complimented me on my cute shoes. It made me feel good. The MS specialist confirmed what we already knew...I have MS. I'm lucky that my case is easily confirmed from their series of tests. I know that many people struggle with getting a confirmed diagnosis, because their test results aren't always textbook. My test results easily check off all the required boxes. This doctor agreed with my current neurologist's course of treatment and I was told to make another appointment if anything changed drastically.

We made the long drive home and I talked the whole way as usual. We walked into the house and my twelve-year-old son immediately noticed my new, bright, stylish tennis shoes.

"Cool shoes, Mom! Maybe people will notice your shoes instead of the way you walk!" he exclaimed.

I stopped, a bit stunned by that comment. My son is very kindhearted and would never be mean. I knew he meant well. But pointing out that people notice how I waddle and lift my foot up with each step at a sloth's pace, stung a little bit.

He continued to smile at me.

Then I laughed. And laughed some more. I could have chosen to be hurt by his statement. I could have felt sorry for myself for how I walk. But he had a good point! Leave it to a boy to say it like it is. I chose to look at it his way.

Maybe people would notice my stylish shoes and not the way I walk. I wore those shoes everywhere. I noticed people looking at me. I walked like a feeble, elderly woman yet in a fairly fit 40-something's body. But then I'd tell myself, "They're just noticing my cool shoes!" and I'd believe it.

Quite often I'd receive compliments from strangers about my cute shoes, so my belief obtained credibility. I began walking with confidence instead of humiliation. I no longer worried about people noticing the way I hobbled because I figured they were just staring at my shoes.

This one little mind game made all the difference. Gone was my embarrassment. In its place was pride. Who knew a simple pair of shoes and a boy's blunt comment could have such an effect?

Take that, Missy. A simple pair of neon-striped shoes overpower you.

Miss Depressed

Having Missy come into my life took away everything I loved to do and that made me *me*. Every muscle in my body hurt every day. I had no stamina to make it through an entire day without rest. My life was consumed by what Missy decided I could and couldn't do.

I cried every day.

Why did this happen to me? What would I do now? I didn't want to be a burden to my family. What will bring joy to my life now? What worth did I possess? What was the point of suffering every day? I had no hope to improve, only to get worse.

I cried every day.

Since I'm married to a counselor, I had no choice but to follow his demand that I take an antidepressant. He's the expert, after all. He could see my depression and worried about me. Telling him that I'd rather be dead probably wasn't the smartest thing to do on my part.

I went to my primary doctor for a prescription for an antidepressant. He had been the one to diagnose me with MS.

"So, you're feeling depressed?" he asked.

"Yep," I replied.

"What's making you depressed?" he asked.

"Well, let's see. I have this brain disease that took away my ability to walk, run, and dance. It takes away

126

my vision. I can't feel anything on half of my body. I can't remember what I did yesterday. I've lost my job and many friends. My future will consist of years of a disabling disease. I guess what's making me depressed is that MS f—king sucks!" I said.

"Alrighty then. Are you suicidal?" he continued with his legal questions.

"Do I wish I could die? Yes. Who wants to live like this? Am I going to kill myself? No. I wouldn't do that to my family." I replied.

"Do you want me to refer you to a counselor?" he asked.

"Nope. Married to one." I answered.

I guess I passed his test because I left with a prescription. Missy was not happy with this. She loved making me miserable. She loved having the power to take away my joy. She enjoyed knowing that along with my suffering body, was my suffering mind.

The last thing I had wanted to do was to take more medications with more potential side effects. We all know that side effects are sometimes worse than the issue the medication is trying to help. The last thing I needed was to be a joyful soul who was confined to a toilet. But I agreed to take something.

Except for some initial stomach upset, side effects were minimal. Within a few weeks, I began noticing that I wasn't crying as much. As time passed, I realized I'd gone several days without feeling like my life had ended.

Was Missy riding my back? Slowing me down? Keeping me in bed? Slapping me around? Yes.

But I no longer felt hopelessly defeated. I was feeling better emotionally.

And what, to therapists' dismay, do people on antidepressants do when they start feeling better? Quit the medication! "I'm better! I don't need it!"

Wrong.

Within a matter of days, I again cried every day. Within a couple of weeks, I was hopeless and wanted to die. Missy was stronger than ever.

Fine. I'll take the medication.

I also found a counselor. After eight straight hours of listening to people cry, grieve, and complain, the last thing my husband needed to come home to was a crying, grieving, and complaining spouse. I knew he cared about me, but using him as my therapist would only drain him. He was helpless. Listening to my suffering only hurt him as well. That is not to say I didn't tell him what was going on or how I felt. I kept him in the loop. I just didn't rely on him to pull me out of my pit of despair.

My weekly crying and complaining sessions were very therapeutic. My counselor was not only empathetic, but also offered good ideas for managing my thoughts and emotions.

When doctors and hospitals hear that I'm on antidepressants, they always ask, "Do you suffer from depression?"

It's such an odd question to me. I don't *suffer* from it because I do something about it. If I didn't treat it, would I suffer? Yes. Do I suffer from a chemical imbalance in my brain that causes depressed feelings? Maybe. Do I have a controlling, vindictive, evil being living in my body who screws up everything I want in my life, causing me to feel depressed? You betcha.

I respond in the affirmative. I've then been asked if I'm disabled due to my depression. No. I'm depressed because I'm disabled.

Medications and counseling help. I don't want these things but since Missy is here to stay, I'll do what I have to do to get along with her.

Park It

Why is it that when you desperately need to find a
restroom, there isn't one to be found? The same goes
for a gas station. The gasoline light goes on and all
nearby gas stations suddenly vanish. Shortly after Missy
became a constant passenger in my car, I discovered
that convenient, and very necessary, parking places also
seemed to disappear into thin air.

I was already fatigued by hauling a piggy-backing Missy
everywhere I went. However, grocery shopping was
something I was determined to do. (Not because I like it.
I usually have two or three items mixed in to a full cart.
But kids and a husband whine like babies when they are
out of the zillion food items they need to survive.)

Knowing that I had to walk a marathon inside that
grocery store, I hoped for a parking place close to the
entrance. It would save a few steps at least.

But after weaving up and down each row, I was stuck
with a place near the farthest-away shopping cart return.

(A light bulb blinked on over my head.) *I have an idea!
Use one of the shopping carts as a walker.*

I could walk a bit farther and more easily with a
walker. But a grocery cart was an incognito walker. I
could nonchalantly stroll into the store while grasping
the handle for balance. Nobody would suspect that
I couldn't walk. They would think I was a regular
shopper, leisurely meandering through the store, without
a care in the world.

They probably wouldn't notice my wobbly legs or the way my left foot dropped with each step. Nobody would know about the muscle aches or the extreme mental processes it took to walk. I talked myself into a buying a cup of Starbucks coffee (which doesn't take a lot of convincing) in order to further my disguise as the content, easy-going shopper who has nowhere else to be.

That charade continued while I tossed each family members' individually selected items into the basket (because nobody likes to eat what the others eat and each requires *their kind* of foods).

By the time I had walked the ten-mile marathon and painstakingly placed each item onto the checkout belt, only to then have to lift and drop all of the bagged items back into my cart, I was kaput.

Thus began the trip across the bumpy parking lot all the way to my car. Because I looked like a healthy, in-shape woman in her 40's, drivers in that parking lot had little sympathy for me. They figured I could stand and wait while they backed out of their parking spaces. I looked healthy enough to let them drive through the crosswalk, instead of allowing me to walk through it first. I certainly did not resemble someone who needed help lifting the trunk of her car or loading the zillion and three plastic bags into it. Thankfully, I'd parked near the cart return and I wobbled back to my car. Once my door was closed, I flopped against my seat in total exhaustion. Time to rest.

After many similar episodes, I began to consider requesting a handicapped-parking placard.

But those are for the elderly and those in wheelchairs. I didn't deserve it. I hadn't earned it. They needed it more than I did.

I had a tender place in my heart for people of all ages with physical disabilities. Since as a child a disease had stunted the growth of one of my legs, I grew up going to a hospital designated for crippled children. At each visit, when I saw those children who struggled far more than I did, I admired them. They had more pain, more to suffer and more to conquer than I did. Yet, they smiled and persevered. For some reason, in the waiting rooms, they'd gravitate to me. They'd want to build blocks with me or read stories with me. My heart would melt, and I always felt honored to spend time with them. I felt a bit guilty that I could walk out of that hospital after each checkup and continue with a normal, active life, while those innocent children were restricted to wheelchairs.

So considering my need for handicapped parking did not come easily.

I decided to mention it to my doctor and gauge his reaction. If he balked and bristled, I'd know I had no business even thinking about it. I'd apologize and quickly explain that I was not one of those people trying to take advantage of a situation.

However, his eyes grew big and he stared at me and said, "You don't have one already?! That's ridiculous! You absolutely require one. I don't know how I missed that. I will fill out the forms right now."

I didn't know whether this was bad news or good news. Bad news: "You're disabled enough to have handicapped-parking." Good news: "You're disabled enough to have handicapped-parking!"

The day I went to the county building to get the placard, I found it ironic that all parking places seemed to be located an uphill mile from the office where handicapped-parking forms needed to be turned in. However, it was all processed and I hobbled out with my blue card.

I promptly shoved it into my glove compartment, determined never to use it.

Then came a day of Missy rearing her evil head. She'd woken up in a foul mood and had decided to take it out on my body by causing it to cramp, twitch, and tighten. It was one of those times when she wanted to pout in bed all day with me. But I needed to run an errand and putting it off was not an option. She came along with me, stomping and grumbling the whole time.

As usual, I circled the rows in the parking lot, hoping for a spot close to the door. Nothing. Missy perked up when she remembered that I had a handicapped-parking card.

"Yes! Let's use your card!" I could imagine her shouting. She seemed to enjoy reminding me of the destruction that she had caused.

I looked at the four empty-handicapped parking spaces that were near the door. I saw an older gentleman quickly swerve his new Corvette into the closest space and rather spryly leap out the door and journey inside.

I was not judging. I was fully aware that not all disabilities are visible. I was, however, *comparing.* In comparison, in that particular moment, I seemed to need a close parking space even more than he did. The words "spry, leap and journey" did not describe my movements that day.

Fine. I'm desperate. I'll just park here once and even then, I'm taking the farthest space in case someone comes along who needs it more than I do.

I begrudgingly parked, hung up my blue card and slowly hobbled into the store. By the time I had gotten what I needed and had waited in line, I found huge relief in knowing that I didn't have a far walk to get to my car. I got in, sat down, and breathed. I'd made it.

From then on, I committed myself to only parking in handicapped spaces if absolutely necessary. I still took the farthest one available, knowing in the back of my mind that someone else might need the closer spaces more than I did.

I doubt many people saw it that way. For some, it seemed they were privileged to park there and they'd use it whether or not they actually needed it. Even worse, some, who have no disabilities whatsoever, illegally park there and feel entitled to the closer parking spaces.

Instead, for me, I am genuinely grateful on days when I feel well enough to park in a regular parking space and can leave those spaces for other deserving people. If I was having a "good day," then I felt blessed for it. Lucky me! I didn't need handicapped-parking that day!

So my blue handicapped-parking placard stays in my glove compartment and is only used on an as-needed basis. Sometimes Missy makes me pull it out and hang it up, and other times she doesn't realize that I've parked in a regular space until it's too late.

I hope that if and when Missy fully takes over and demands the need for special parking to accommodate our wheelchair, other people in that parking lot will think like I did and not only save those places for people who truly need it, but will also be grateful that they don't.

Missy's Kryptonite Attack

I am a very even-keeled person. I don't get mad easily. I don't hold grudges. I don't really have a temper. I'm neither overly passionate about things nor annoyingly excitable. I'm pretty much always in a content mood. (Putting this in writing makes me seem rather boring, but I always felt proud that I was this way.)

However, being told that I had yet another active lesion on my brain, causing yet another flare up, with yet more annoying symptoms, always meant that Missy would get to inflict more evil and discomfort through intravenous medication. Steroids. It's her form of kryptonite. She knows using it on me will cause significant side effects, resulting in complete and unpleasant incapacitation. She might as well just use a long-lasting stun gun.

Many times steroids are required to be given intravenously over 3-5 days. I've experienced this through both hospitalizations and home health care. To me, getting an IV isn't traumatic. Other than a metallic taste in my mouth, I can't feel the powerful liquid enter my veins. I've understood from the very beginning that high dose steroids are the typical protocol for a flare up. I have to accept that. But here's why it's my nemesis: It essentially killed my mother at the age of 56.

My mother was steroid-dependent due to severe, chronic asthma. She literally could not breathe without steroid medication. She tried many times to get off of them, but when she could not inhale and exhale enough air to stay alive, what was the point? I watched steroids cause her to have glaucoma in her eyes. She had osteoporosis in her bones from the long-term use, which meant she suffered from chronic pain, and she required surgeries to try to repair the damage to her bones. Her skin was like taut tissue paper. A mere tap or bump would cause her skin to burst open into a gaping wound. Stitches were impossible because the thread would tear through the skin. Ultimately, I watched how long-term, high-dose steroids destroyed her immune system to the point that it no longer existed. She died from not being able to fight off infections.

So Missy came into my life and what is the one remedy doctors have to stop her brain invasions? High-dose steroids! Yippee! The "cure-all." Obviously, I do not take these drugs lightly. At first, I wanted to outright refuse. But, as it's the only way to combat Missy, I agree to it sometimes. She has the potential to cause irreparable damage more so than a round of medications.

However, Missy finds it absolutely hilarious that the one drug I have to take to knock her off her high horse, just happens to make me miserable in the process.

I empathize with people who have hyperactivity or uncontrollable energy. That's what steroids do to me.

Oh look at that closet! Why, I should take everything out of it, sort through it, organize it and put it back in! And that closet, too! And that pantry! And that cabinet! What do you mean it's after midnight? I'm full of energy! Who needs to sleep? I wanna get things done! Fine. I'll go to bed. Gosh, my body is buzzin' and hummin'. When will it be morning?

I got up in the morning and I spilled coffee grounds on the countertop.

"What the heck?! That's it! I **hate** coffee!! I will **never** drink it again. Who invented that stuff anyway? I want to have a serious talk with them. I **hate** them. If my husband hadn't introduced me to coffee, this never would have happened. You know what? I **hate** him too! Why the heck can I not scoop up these coffee grounds? What is **wrong** with them?!" I shout, mutter, and fume. To myself. Because nobody else was in the room. And it's a good thing because if I even *saw* a living being, I would probably rip off its head.

*Annnddd...*that is me on steroids. Missy finds humor in watching such an even-tempered woman as myself experience a violent streak a mile wide. I could throw knives, kick kittens and verbally describe to someone where the "sun don't shine" because steroids have a way of removing my filter and making my blood boil at the same time.

When I realized that I had terrified my family, (who proceeded to look up "local exorcist" on Yelp) my mood shifted again and I became a sorrowful, bawling mess begging for forgiveness. Hyperventilating through sobs, I reminded them to have patience with me because I'm on steroids.

Then, just like that, "Who's hungry? I'm starving! Let's go eat! Hurry! I might die waiting for you. Can we go to Chipotle, Pizza Hut *and* Chick fil-A because all of it sounds good and I feel like I haven't eaten in years. Hurry up! I'm dying!" My family silently marched to the car wondering who was this off-kilter, off-meds and off-the-wagon psych ward resident, because it couldn't be their wife or mother.

An Entertaining Way to Cope

Missy was in the corner, snacking on popcorn, enjoying the show.

Once I was home, I looked in the mirror and noticed a thousand prepubescent pimples covering my entire face, as well as a five-month-pregnant belly. Having seen it before, I knew it would take the better part of five months for that belly to return to normal size. I was instantly in rage mixed with melt-down.

And all because I required high-dose steroids to stop the brain damage that the mighty, powerful Missy was causing. She never seemed to mind the fact that her ultimate mission was squelched before maximum damage could be done, because she was so thoroughly entertained by the whole process.

Nightmare

Once Missy had attacked my vision, a nightmare that I'd had most of my adult life seemed to be coming true. Being that I was already blind in one eye, it was my biggest fear to lose sight in my other eye. Missy chose my left occipital lobe in my brain in order to damage the vision in my right eye. I'd lose sight in it for a matter of minutes to hours, often daily or several times a week.

I'm very close to my daughter. I'd always dreamed of having a little girl. It just so happened that she is a new and improved, perfected mini-me. We look alike, sound alike, think alike and talk alike. Of course, I find her to be superior in intelligence, drive, beauty, and success. Sure, we'd butt heads, disagree and struggle over who was in control, but we could also spend hours laughing our tails off in a dressing room, singing the lead and backups of Aretha Franklin's *Respect* and banding together against the boys in the house.

She went through the typical teenage stage of trying to say to me, "Don't tell me what to do." I'd calmly respond with, "I will always tell you what to do." Since she was a well-behaved teenager, she'd frequently use that phrase to be funny. I'd say, "Have a good day!" and she'd reply, "Don't tell me what to do!" to which I'd reply, "I will always tell you what to do!" It became a phrase between us as special as "I love you."

I remember the dream vividly. Bustling around in a sunlit room with various activity and chatter going on around us. There was excitement in the air and joy in our hearts. It was my daughter's wedding day, and we were all in a room getting ready. Hairspray filled the room along with the sound of bridesmaids' high heels. I was sitting in awe with all the commotion around me. Suddenly, I was told that it was "time" and I was helped up from where I'd sat. This was when I realized during the dream that I was blind. I was escorted to where my daughter was dressed in her wedding gown with her veil, hair and make-up perfect for a bride. I instinctively reached my hands up to feel her veil, her hair and her face in order to "see" my daughter dressed as a bride. I had to use my sense of touch to imagine what she looked like on that special day. It broke my heart.

I woke up crying. Aloud, I begged God and even Missy to never allow that dream, that nightmare, to come true. In the back of my mind, I worried that Missy was even more powerful than God himself, and that she'd find pleasure in taking that special moment, among others, away from me. Not only was I terrified of becoming blind and terrified of having that dream come true, I was even terrified of having that dream again.

But a few years later? I have peace. The longer I live with Missy, the more things come into perspective. It reminds me of a technique I use on myself, and even family and friends. Worst Case Scenario. We are afraid of the worst possible thing that can happen. But if we allow our minds to go *there* and explore what we fear, then we are able to gather Intel. What *if* that horrible thing happens? What will I do? How will I feel? How will I recover?

It's awful and frightening to think about. But more often than not, I discover that a plan of action *does* exist and I *will* be okay. Knowing this, lessens the fear.

So my biggest fear, even more so than losing my ability to walk, is Missy taking my sight. The thought of not seeing my daughter on her wedding day, my son graduate from college, the unique amber of my husband's eyes or even the beauty of my future grandchildren is incredibly sad, and I hope that doesn't happen.

But if it does, I will be okay. I always am. We will figure out how to make the best of it. I will be determined to focus on the joy of the occasion. Because, I am not going to allow Missy to make me live in fear. Although she thinks she is some boogeyman dressed in black and a ski mask who steals sight, balance, sensation and vocabulary when I least expect it, I will not fear her. She doesn't deserve that much power.

I will be okay. I always am. Besides, fear of the future only drains today of its joy.

Missy

I've accepted that Missy is a part of my life. I have developed a symbiotic relationship with her. I accept that she will never leave me alone nor go away. I've accepted that she will be a constant companion, and that she has the ability to cause extreme damage both physically and mentally.

I've learned the hard way that I cannot ignore her. I've realized that hating her and getting angry at her, seems to give her more power to cause me fatigue and additional pain. I know she can cause great sadness and can take away things in my life that bring me joy.

I know that *she* is the cause of my disability, my fatigue, my weak legs, my vision loss and my sketchy memory. It's not that I did something to cause it, nor that I have the ability to overcome it.

She moved in and turned my life upside down. She forced me to change my habits, my likes and dislikes, my routines, and even my dreams. She is time-consuming, thought-consuming and identity-consuming. She is enmeshed in every thought and decision I make, from when and how to get out of bed each morning, to what legacy I want to leave at the end of my life.

The best thing I ever did was separate her from me. In order to continue to have power, joy and self-worth, I needed her to be a separate entity. When I did this, everything changed. I was able to see myself as Janelle, not Janelle-with-MS. I could picture myself living life as *me,* with Missy tagging along beside me, instead of as a disease-ridden human.

I could still laugh and even have joy and adventure. I could learn how to do new things and create new goals for my life. With Missy being separate and apart from me, I took my life back...and she would simply be joining me.

This concept changed the way my family saw me as well.

Instead of, "How are you feeling today?" the question would be, "What's Missy up to today?" This meant I no longer had to evaluate what I was feeling or try to soften my words to avoid scaring or saddening them.

I could respond with, "She's fairly calm today and not bothering me too much." Or, "She is literally on my nerves today. She's playing games with my vision and balance."

This helped my family to see my illness as a separate entity. It also gave them "someone" to hate and direct their anger towards, instead of some imaginary amoeba-looking disease. It's not uncommon around my house to hear phrases like, "That darn Missy. Look what she made you do..." and "I guess Missy wants you to rest today so let's just watch a movie." And even, "I hate Missy so much. I hate what she does to you." We even give Missy credit for some of the humorous things I do, "Ha-ha! Missy must've been drinking because she's making you slur your words!"

It's helpful for me to picture her annoying blond ringlets, crooked teeth and frumpy clothes and then roll my eyes at her, not letting her intimidate me. Sometimes she's bossy and I have to do what she says or suffer severe consequences. Other times, I try to compromise with her and she often allows me to have my way. Every once in a while, under special circumstances, I stand up to her, fight her or ignore her and understand that she'll demand one-on-one time with me the next day. I choose the times that are worth paying that price. Believe it or not, there have even been times I've come to appreciate her existence in my life. Certain things wouldn't have occurred if she hadn't been hanging around. I'll cherish those moments for the rest of my life. (Don't get me wrong. She's more than welcome to pack her bags and move on anytime she wants to.)

For therapeutic reasons, I've shouted at her. I've expressed what I truly think of her. I've begged her and pleaded with her. I've cried about her. I've had conversations with her to keep her identity separate from mine. I've stood up to her. I've taunted and teased her. I've rubbed it in when she had failed in her attempts to ruin yet another thing in my life. I've even quietly and sincerely thanked her for teaching me what's important in my life.

I will do my best to get along with Missy for the rest of my life. I find comfort in the knowledge that "people" like her won't have the pleasure of joining me in Heaven.

Moment of Joy

I wake up stiff and sore. I'm immediately reminded that I can't feel my left side. I notice that my lips are tingling. Is Missy up to something new?

I mentally plan my day. *Go make coffee. Sit and rest while I drink it. Take a shower. Lie down to watch a TV show. Take the dog on a walk. Lie back down. Make some phone calls while lying down again. Pick up my son from school and take him to practice. Start dinner while resting in between tasks, etc.*

Every single activity requires constant, purposeful mental thought to make my body do what I need it to do. Every single activity drains my low battery, and I am required to recharge it between activities. Every single activity brings pain from muscle fatigue, spasticity, and weakness. Some activities, other than the "resting" ones, fail to be accomplished.

And I know that when I get into bed at night, my entire body will be tense, shaky and in pain. And I know that I will have to do it all over again the next day.

What a life. Or rather, a life *sentence.*

I'm assuming that prisoners serving life sentences, incarcerated inside cement walls, have to invent ways to get through each day without going insane or committing suicide. I needed to do the same because I was a prisoner as well. Life with Missy was certainly a life sentence confined by boundaries.

It was an early summer's day. I'd decided to spend it with my son to celebrate the end of his school year. We had chosen to go to our local river walk to ride paddleboats and then to enjoy pizza, his favorite food, at a restaurant overlooking the river.

We arrived at the river walk and rented a paddleboat. I figured this was a perfect activity because when my legs grew tired, my son could pedal for me. We put on the faded, old-fashioned life vests and climbed into the red two-seated boat. It took us a while to figure out how to maneuver the boxy contraption. We'd laugh when we went left but wanted to go right. We hit a literal wall and took forever trying to figure out how to turn around. We stopped to take selfies (only because I made him). Missy was sharing my seat, so sometimes she insisted that my legs rest while my strong boy pedaled hard enough to haul both of us around. We pedaled around and around until our time was up.

We headed toward the dock and had obviously improved our maneuvering skills, because we coasted into the slot rather successfully. The attendant came to my side to help me climb out of the boat and onto the dock. As I was holding the guy's hand and gingerly stepping onto the shaky wooden dock, watching my feet cooperate with my task at hand...I heard a splash.

I whipped around to find my son chest-deep in the water on his side of the paddleboat. He had a death grip with both hands on the edge of it and somehow, one foot was still aboard. His knee on that leg was right next his face.

I immediately asked a stupid question, "What are you doing?!"

"You threw me out!" he shouted, while trying to figure a way out of his situation.

"What?" I asked, trying to figure out how to help him.

Do I climb back into the boat? Why isn't the attendant helping? Oh my gosh, he looks hilarious like that.

I burst out laughing. And laughing and laughing. Laughing so hard I wasn't breathing or making any sound. Then a snort found its way out as I inhaled while laughing.

Meanwhile, he hoisted himself over the edge of the boat and onto his stomach. He pulled himself out of the water and stood up. He was sopping wet. Wet shirt, one wet leg of his shorts and one dripping sock and tennis shoe.

He immediately started to blame me, "Mom! When you stood up, so did I. When you got out, the weight shifted on the boat and threw me off the other side!!"

My laughter turned into all-out-roaring laughter after I pictured the boat dipping down on my side as I exited then launching him into the water as my weight left the boat. I remembered the way he was hanging on for dear life and then looked again at his sopping wet clothes. Fortunately, he was then to the point of laughing along with me. The attendant stood awkwardly and smiled.

That's when it hit me. When I was laughing and enjoying an experience, I was able to put Missy in a quiet, dark corner. I had enjoyed a Missy-free moment. I didn't feel her. I didn't hear her. I was enjoying and noting the present moment. I decided to hang on to that memory.

That night, as I went to bed feeling all of the usual fatigue, aches and pains, I recalled my son having been catapulted into the water after my plentiful tushy left the paddleboat, and how he clung to the side with his knee up by his face and I laughed. The silent chuckle the wife is supposed to laugh in order not to wake her sleeping husband next to her. But that never works. My laughter increased and I began shaking the bed. My voice croaked as I inhaled and laughed...thus, waking my husband. Fortunately, he seemed pleased to wake to my laughter rather than my frequent tears, so he joined in my replaying the hilarious event. I eventually drifted off to sleep with a smile on my face. I decided to try to make that happen every night.

After that day, I remained on the lookout for my daily "moment of joy." I didn't force it to happen. I simply waited throughout the day and eventually, something would be said or done that would trigger a "This is it" feeling. I'd consciously be aware to revel in that feeling as long as possible (it would be the one time during my day that Missy was seemingly absent) and to note it so I could use it again as I fell asleep that night.

Usually my moments of joy are something that a family member or friend does or says that makes me burst out laughing. They have quick wits that catch me off-guard. Sometimes my moment of joy is a milestone such as a kid's graduation, performance or sporting event. A moment of joy with my husband might include how I felt when he kissed me (Missy is *never* a part of moments like that), or late at night when we should be trying to sleep and we end up making each other laugh hysterically about something nobody else would find funny. I've even had moments of joy with strangers. Maybe a pleasurable conversation with a fellow line-waiter at the coffee shop, or I surprised a stranger with a compliment or good deed, and I'm left with that warm feeling. Other times, it's just a few seconds of laughter brought on by friends, family, strangers, the radio or the television.

I never know when, where, or how I will experience my moment of joy, but they give me a reason to get up every morning. I have yet to have a day without one. And every night, I fall asleep remembering one.

My life has become a series of cherished joyful moments. Moments that wouldn't have been noticed or appreciated had Missy not come into my life. If I work hard at getting along with Missy, I'm still given a life of joy.

Follow "Missy and Me" on Facebook at:

www.facebook.com/authorjsims

And go to:

www.GettingAlongWithMissy.com

For updated blogs

Watch for the workbook titled
The Making of Missy
Coming Soon!

Acknowledgments

Writing a book is a long process that requires the gifts, support, and efforts of many people.

To my precious circle of friends: This was your idea! It figures that a group of educators would prompt me to write a book. Thank you for encouraging me throughout this process. Thank you especially to Barb and Lareen for helping with the photography on my cover. To lose my identity as a teacher was one of the hardest parts of this journey. The fear of losing my dear teaching friends was an added heartache. But that didn't happen. You have rallied around me, helped me, prayed for me, and most importantly, have been a source of laughter, adventure and joy. I'm blessed to call you friends and fellow members of the I-Hate-Missy Club.

To my cousin, Dawn Eddy: Who would've thought, back during our childhood of riding horses, road trips in the mountains and sharing family holidays, that one day you would design the cover of my book? (Notice, I left out mentioning our teen years of driving to school together and sharing a few boyfriends.) It has been fun to go through this process with you. You have such an eye for design and it's as if you could read my mind when it came to the cover of this book. I love you, cousin.

To my fellow educator and book-lover Maureen Seals: I knew the minute we met that you were the perfect person to edit my book. Allowing someone to change a very personal work from my soul takes real trust. I doubt Picasso let anyone add or remove strokes on his artwork. But you had a way of perfecting my writing while maintaining my voice. You were able to enter my imagination and interpret the meaning behind my words. Not only that, your pleasure from reading my story brought such encouragement. Thank you for your hard work and expertise.

To one of my favorite students, Mason Goode: My teaching career did not last near as long as I wanted it to. So, I've chosen to cherish the memories I *was* able to create. You are one of them. I loved that you didn't fit into the box of other students. Your quick wit made me laugh daily. Your creativity inspired me. Your unique way of learning and producing challenged me. And this is why, when I needed pictures drawn of Missy and me, the boy who drew cartoons in the back of my classroom, instead of doing his work, came to my mind. Thank you for stepping out of your comfort zone and allowing me to have a piece of your gift of art. It will always be something I cherish.

To my son, Keaton: If it weren't for Missy, I wouldn't have been able to devote as much time to you the last few years. Missy forced me to recognize my priorities and you *for sure* are one of them. I am so blessed to have such an intelligent, patient, compassionate, easy-going son. I'm so thankful that God gave me a boy, even when I didn't think I wanted one. Without you, I never would have learned so much about sports, cars, and machining. And I never would have known what it's like for a mother to love a son. Thank you for helping me when Missy is being a pain. Thank you for laughing with me when she makes me feel stupid. And thank you for being proud of a mom who sometimes uses a cane and a handicapped card. You are more precious to me than you will ever understand.

To my daughter, Kyndal: You are so much more than the little girl I always wanted. You have brought experiences to my life that I never would have fathomed. It was bittersweet to see my daughter grow up in front of my eyes when Missy moved in. I was proud of how you stepped up to take on the role of woman-of-the-house with such confidence and knowledge. One of the things that keeps me going is the excitement of witnessing you living your best life. I love you, my sweet girl.

Saving the best for last, to my husband, Greg: Throughout our years together, you have continually moved the boundaries of my comfort zone. By giving me ideas farther than my imagination could have reached coupled with copious amounts of encouragement, praise and faith, I was able to write this book. Your confidence in my ability gave me the confidence I needed. Thank you for reading every word aloud to me so that I could hear how it sounded. Thank you for laughing and crying in the parts it warranted. But most importantly, thank you for choosing to ride this rollercoaster with Missy and me. You are there for the ups, downs, laughter, screams, hope, and fear on these twists and turns, and I wouldn't survive without you buckled in the seat next to me. And when this ride comes to a stop, I will have such comfort knowing that I was blessed to marry the man of my dreams. My one true love. My best friend and soul mate. You will always have my heart.

Made in the USA
Middletown, DE
11 April 2022

63778947R00099